THE
BIG
GAMBLE

THE
BIG
GAMBLE

The Politics of
Lottery and Casino Expansion

Denise von Herrmann

Westport, Connecticut
London

Library of Congress Cataloging-in-Publication Data

Von Herrmann, Denise, 1962–
    The big gamble : the politics of lottery and casino expansion / Denise von Herrmann.
        p.   cm.
    Includes bibliographical references and index.
    ISBN 0–275–97750–1 (alk. paper)
    1. Gambling—Government policy—United States.   2. Gambling industry—Government policy—United States.   3. Lotteries—United States.   4. Casinos—United States.   I. Title.
    HV6715.V77   2002
    363.4'2'0973—dc21   2002067299

British Library Cataloguing in Publication Data is available.

Library of Congress Catalog Card Number: 2002067299
ISBN: 0–275–97750–1

First published in 2002

Praeger Publishers, 88 Post Road West, Westport, CT 06881
An imprint of Greenwood Publishing Group, Inc.
www.praeger.com

Printed in the United States of America

∞™

The paper used in this book complies with the Permanent Paper Standard issued by the National Information Standards Organization (Z39.48–1984).

10 9 8 7 6 5 4 3 2 1

Contents

Tables

Acknowledgments

In every large undertaking such as this, there are many persons who provide assistance and support along the way. I would be remiss if I did not take the time to thank some of them. Two colleagues at The University of Southern Mississippi (USM) collaborated with me on a statewide study of gaming in 1999 and 2000: Robert Ingram and William Smith provided valuable insights into the industry and helped me to find not only data and resources, but also a greater degree of interdisciplinary thinking in my approach to the topic. Likewise, Greg Bradley and John Brady of Decision Scientific, industry professionals who served as consultants to that same study, took the time to share their experience and knowledge with an academic. Dr. Lowell Goodman, another study consultant, provided both data and assistance. Of course the Mississippi Institutions of Higher Learning, and especially Dr. Phil Pepper, also deserve thanks for the opportunity to work on that important public policy project.

I am grateful to Dr. Patrick Cotter at the University of Alabama, for his clear thoughts and for sharing his data. Two of his colleagues, Dr. John Bolland and Dr. Steven Borelli, also helped shape the content for many of these pages. Researchers at the Eagleton Poll provided important data and were very helpful. Research librarians at the University of Nevada Las Vegas library, as well as those at my home institution, USM, assisted greatly in finding research and data.

My graduate assistants at USM, Dan Slusher and Kathy Thompson, provided much appreciated data entry and bibliographic work. Two anonymous reviewers' detailed and insightful reading of an early draft of the manuscript helped me hone portions of it into a much more concise and readable document. Much of their contribution was the extent to which I replied to their criticisms by focusing more clearly upon why I was writing, and I am grateful for their blunt and honest appraisal. I am also grateful for the assistance of Dr. James T. Sabin and the fine editorial staff at Greenwood Publishers, who have truly been as helpful and supportive as any author could want.

Finally, I am compelled to thank the many scholars from a variety of disciplines who have shared their work in the area of gambling policy. Their data collections, analysis, and insights into the nature and effects of all forms of gambling have been invaluable in informing my ongoing inquiry into this fascinating policy area.

1

Introduction: Policy Making and Morals

Why write a public policy book about gambling? Is there anything important about gambling that we do not already know? While the gambling industry is indisputably large and powerful (having generated some $54.4 billion in 1999), it has not received much attention from political scientists. Of the two dozen or so scholarly[1] books that have been published about the industry, most are either purely historical or take a sociological approach. A political scientist joined with a sociologist to publish a book on casino adoptions (Dombrink & Thompson, 1990), and there have been only a dozen or so scholarly articles in the political science and public policy journals. Obviously, there is still much to learn about the politics of gambling.

A 1999 congressionally funded gambling study showed that gambling activity has increased among U.S. households: In 1975 one out of every three adults reported having "never gambled," whereas in 1999 that number had dropped to just one in seven adults (National Opinion Research Center [NORC], 1999). More people appear to have gambled, but most are not necessarily doing so more often. The percentage of persons who report having gambled at least once in 1999 was almost identical to the percentage reporting doing so in 1976: 63 percent versus 61 percent. The games of choice have changed dramatically since 1975; the number of patrons of casinos and lotteries has increased, whereas the number of patrons for bingo and horse racing has declined (NORC, 1999).

The surveys also considered the age of gamblers, and here important differences emerge between 1975 and 1999. In the earlier study, about 75 percent of young people (those aged 18–24) reported having ever gambled, whereas only 35 percent of older people (those 65 and older) reported doing so. By 1999, lifetime gambling was up only slightly (to 80 percent) in the younger group, but was up sharply (now at 80 percent) among the elderly.

While it might be tempting to surmise that gambling is now more politically popular, this would be an incomplete portrayal of the current situation. Between 1994 and 1997, 11 out of 17 gambling referenda were defeated in states throughout the United States. Casinos or expansions of existing casino legislation were rejected in Arkansas, Colorado, Florida, Ohio, Rhode Island, and Washington in 1994 and 1995 ("Gambling Under Attack," 1996). Bruising political battles were fought in the state legislatures of two southern states (Alabama and South Carolina) over lotteries in 1998, and lottery proponents carried the day in both states. However, Alabama Governor Don Siegelman and other lottery supporters were stunned when the lottery was soundly defeated in a 1999 referendum.

"Gambling is perhaps the most widely misunderstood activity of economic significance in the United States," according to Eugene Christiansen (1998, p. 37). It is also widely misunderstood in terms of its political significance. The key to describing why it is generally misunderstood lies in an examination of the history and status of gambling policy within a morality policy process framework.

MORALITY POLITICS AS A GENRE

A recent body of work addresses a burgeoning subfield that interests many political scientists, policy analysts, policy makers, and students of politics in general. "Morality policy," as it is commonly called, encompasses a wide-ranging spectrum of political concerns from abortion and gay rights to euthanasia, drugs and alcohol, prostitution, and gambling (Studlar, 2001). Central questions tie these seemingly disparate areas of public policy together: Should the state be making policy in this area? Should the state ever profit from the "sin" of its citizens? Is it enough to simply outlaw certain kinds of immoral behavior, or should the state vigorously enforce its morality laws?

"The definition of what qualifies as morality policy lies not in any intrinsic, objective characteristic of a policy or the substantive topic. . . . A policy is classified as a morality policy or not based on the *perceptions* of the actors involved and the terms of debate among them" (Mooney, 2001, p. 4). Morality policies, then, can be distinguished by debate over first principles—arguments that are presented as self-evident, and that lead to "ultimate clashes of values that cannot be resolved by argument" (Black, 1974, p. 23). When clashes between these core values create conflict—such as when Protestant fundamentalists believe that gambling is sinful and persons of other faiths believe gambling is a benign form of entertainment—then political activity becomes necessary to codify the prevailing value (Studlar, 2001).

As the chapters that follow will show, this has happened in the case of gambling policy. While there have been a number of historical cycles of growth in the various forms of gambling, there have also been cycles of reduction and outright prohibition. In order to gamble at a casino in 1988, for example, one had to travel to Nevada or to Atlantic City, New Jersey. Today, at least one form of legal gambling is readily available to most U.S. citizens. By the late 1990s, casino resorts across the country were marketing themselves as fun, *family* vacation spots. How did the transformation occur, and what will it mean for politics and policy?

A POLICY PROCESS FRAMEWORK FOR STUDYING GAMBLING POLICY

As one form of morality policy, gambling should provide evidence of clear distinctions on issues of morals and values. It should have clearly defined support and opposition coalitions, and actors who understand the first principles that underlie its discussion. This book will show that these presuppositions are met in current gambling policies.

However, gambling must also be studied within a consistent and cohesive analytical framework. In his 1971 classic, *A Pre-View of Policy Sciences*, Harold Lasswell argues that all types of policy can be understood within a policy process framework that includes discussion of seven key issues, which I address briefly in the following paragraphs. Yet, applying this rational process approach to gambling—which is inherently a policy arena of competing values, incomplete information, and other paradoxes—is likely to gloss over other important issues at the heart of gambling policy. Our morality policy process model will utilize Lasswell's general framework and structure, while implicitly examining the metaphors (Stone, 1997) that underlie this values-based policy.

The seven key issues I will examine throughout this volume begin with *Who are the participants?* Today the gambling industry is a well-financed, multibillion dollar industry. In 1997, *Fortune* magazine named Mirage Resorts the second most admired corporation, right behind American business icon Coca-Cola. During the 1990s, gambling was the fastest growing industry, expanding at an average rate of 10 percent annually during the early part of the decade (Truitt, 1997, p. 127).

Political figures on both ends of the ideological spectrum have participated in the expansion of gambling. Chapters 2 and 4 detail how Republican elected officials have led many of the recent attacks on gambling, yet many of their compatriots, including Republican Senate Minority Leader Trent Lott, have been both supporters and beneficiaries of the industry.

What expectations and beliefs do the participants in gambling policy bring to the policy process? There was a time when the public was not particularly interested in gambling, although, generally, public sentiment was in opposition to most forms of it. Initially, gambling was widely "stigmatized" (Preston, Bernhard, Hunter, & Bybee, 1998, p. 186). Today, some assert that it is accepted as a "normal part" of people's lives (Rose, 1996).

How, when, where, and how often do the gambling policy participants interact? Gambling policy is largely, although not entirely, state policy. As Chapters 2 and 3 explain, most gambling policy regulation falls within the rubric of the "police powers" clause of the 10th Amendment. Even Indian Gaming, authorized and regulated under the aegis of the Indian Gaming Regulatory Act (IGRA), involves significant participation by state governments as they negotiate tribal compacts to determine the scope and ground rules that will govern specific tribal facilities. Chapter 2 will show, however, that the federal government historically has engaged, and will continue to engage, in various gambling regulation as well.

What resources do the gambling policy participants possess? Gambling is a multibillion dollar industry in the United States. In 1998 alone, Americans gambled some $54 billion at various legal gambling venues (Christiansen, 1999). As with any large industry, gambling interests are well versed in the language and ways of regulatory politics. Industry lobbyists contribute millions of dollars to various political candidates, spend hundreds of thousands more on various political campaigns to legalize or expand gambling opportunities, and are actively involved in every step of the regulatory process. Kindt describes how casino proponents hired 48 lobbyists and spent between $820,000 and $1.1 million during a 45-day legislative session in Virginia in 1995 (1998, p. 86). Yet, with all of the resources of such a large industry behind them, pro-gambling interests have failed repeatedly, as noted earlier.

What strategies do gambling policy participants employ? The gambling industry has, obviously, sought to downplay any perceived negative consequences of gambling while promoting the positive outcomes. However, state governments have been (perhaps unwitting) coconspirators in the attempt to upgrade gambling's image. Since New Hampshire's first state-run lottery in 1964, states have tended to promote gambling heavily as a form of painless tax or a way to export taxes. For the lotteries, wholly owned and operated by the state, that has usually been enough to quiet much of the opposition.

Ever since New Jersey residents first voted on a proposal to authorize casinos in 1974, a proposal that failed to win enough support at the polls (Dombrink & Thompson, 1990, p. 28), a number of states[2] have upped the ante and have tied potential gambling revenues to some target programs such as education, the elderly, or expanded services for the handicapped. When New Jersey took such an approach and tied votes for the casino to support for elderly and handicapped programs, the voters responded with majority approval. Dozens of other states have followed suit: On referenda for lotteries, riverboat casinos, and video-gambling terminals, voters have been told that a vote for gambling is a vote to support increased funding for the designated worthy cause.

What specific benefits do gambling policy participants expect to achieve? A major consideration for gambling policy is the potential impacts of gambling on the larger economy: Gambling has increasingly been presented to the public in economic development terms, which further moves gambling debates from traditional questions of morality. Casinos are the latest and best example of this trend. Especially in poor or economically depressed areas such as Tunica, Mississippi, or downtown Detroit, Michigan, casinos are discussed in terms of the new jobs they will create, the new tourists they will attract, and the potential development of associated amenities such as hotels, golf courses, and restaurants that they will bring.

This economic incentive may be a critical missing piece of the puzzle regarding when, and where, gambling will be adopted. A specific economic need (or the ability to create an impression of economic need in the minds of voters) is critical to the success of gambling campaigns, and it is critical to the ongoing efforts to expand the number and size of gambling outlets.

Finally, *what are the longer-term consequences of the desired outcomes of gambling policy?* Casino gambling, for instance, tends to capture its regulatory bureaucracy and to create a political support network, which serves to further support its entrenchment in society. This further sets gambling policy apart from most observed studies of morality policy. As Meier explains, "The bureaucracies involved in sin policy are law enforcement bureaucracies. . . . Morality bureaucracies produce arrests and expect to be rewarded on the basis of the volume of arrests made" (2001, p. 24). In such an environment, bureaucracies can be expected to push for stronger laws and increased enforcement resources. The industry is not expected to have influence over the policy implementation and reformulation processes (Meier, 1994, p. 246).

Yet, in the case of gambling, Meier's theory does not hold true. As explained in Chapter 5, state gaming commissions have evidenced a propensity to work with the gambling industry to promote expanded access to gambling and, at the same time, have worked to limit the success of any attempts by politicians[3] to mitigate possible negative effects of gambling expansion, all under the goal of maximizing state revenue.

The implications for state politics are important, given that many people still view gambling as stigmatized behavior. Elected state leaders and appointed gambling officials in the lottery and gaming divisions must continue the process of relabeling and destigmatizing gambling. The implications for other areas of morality policy are obvious: If gambling can be relabeled as "family entertainment," then pornography can be relabeled as "alternative entertainment choice," and sodomy laws can be relabeled as "government intrusion into private sexual activity," and so forth. Thus, studying the process by which gambling has managed to shift itself from the category of "sin" to the category of "leisure activity" is instructive to all scholars of public policy.

The remainder of this book includes a careful examination of the legal gambling industry: its history, political impacts, regulation, perceived economic and social impacts, and future. Along the way, primarily the two major forms of gambling that generate the most revenues for state governments will be considered. Examples will be drawn from lotteries and casinos in a number of U.S. states, with special attention paid to the similarities and differences in the political, legal, and regulatory situations that apply to each.

NOTES

1. This number excludes the many textbooks and books for practitioners, which focus mostly on casino management and casino operations.

2. It could be argued here that the gambling industry is the primary mover of policy. Yet, the early history of gambling adoptions suggests that it has typically been state legislators, eager to avoid tax increases, who have turned to gambling as a revenue source. Industry involvement and pressure came later, following the substantial growth in the size and financial influence of that industry that came because of increased legalization of gambling.

3. In this volume, I do not evaluate the merits of these attempts. It is likely that many—for example daily limits on losses, riverboat "cruising" requirements, and the like—might not significantly limit any of these negative social impacts. For the purposes of this discussion, however, it is important only to note the tendency of the bureaucracy to side with industry on such matters.

2

The History and Regulation of Gambling in the United States

Lotteries, casinos, and pari-mutuels, including the various forms of off-track betting, generate substantial revenues for the states that allow them. Some legal forms of gambling do not generate significant revenues for most state or local governments, including Indian gaming, bingo, and raffles. There are also variations on a single theme across states: for instance, a state such as California chooses to authorize card rooms only; another state such as Iowa chooses to allow riverboats; and still another state such as New Jersey allows land-based casino resorts. These gambling forms are very different in terms of access, growth potential, and regulations. Clear distinctions can be drawn between the politics of state lotteries and the politics of casinos, which political scientists and policy researchers have tended to downplay.

LOTTERIES

The gambling phenomenon in the United States is certainly not new. The earliest widespread legal gambling activity in the United States was the lottery. In the 1700s and 1800s, lotteries were a common source of revenue. Most of the earliest lotteries were run by schools and towns in an effort to raise funds for specific uses such as capital construction projects. By the early part of the nineteenth century, though, abuse and fraud became increasing problems. The women's movement and social reformers in the mid-nineteenth century began to use legal gambling activities as a target (often they linked their discussion of gambling to calls for temperance). Many of these groups also had strong ties to churches, and soon Protestants became vocal in their opposition to lotteries (Ezell, 1960, p. 65).

The states began to enter the fight to curb abuse, and eventually legislatures began to pass laws banning lotteries. When the Louisiana lottery was rocked by a mail fraud scandal in the mid-1800s, demands for reform ensued, and states began banning lotteries via statute or constitutional amendment at a greatly hastened pace. As of the close of the nineteenth century, 36 states had constitutional bans on lotteries (Ezell, 1960, p. 239).

One long-lasting effect of this has been that today lotteries are owned and operated by the state itself, rather than by private industry. According to several researchers who have conducted a long-term sociological study of commercial gambling in the United States: "State ownership and operation of lotteries is a legacy of the nineteenth-century scandals involving state-franchised private lotteries: the laws prohibiting them remained in force, and formed the statutory background for modern lottery initiatives. No legislature has been eager to invite repetition of the preceding century's experience with private lottery companies" (Abt, Smith, & Christiansen, 1985, p. 63).

Following the morality policy process framework, an important question is: Who participates in lottery policy today, and what expectations and beliefs do they bring to the process? State lawmakers are one set of actors, yet most have no desire to repeat the disastrous failure of their predecessors in their attempts at legal prohibition of generally accepted social vices. It is likely that public pressure to repeal the alcohol prohibition imposed by the 18th Amendment created a long-lasting impression on the minds of legislators, who now appear quite happy to put such issues before the voters. Of the more than 30 such votes held in the states between 1964 and 1999, only a handful has failed (Clotfelter, Cook, Edell, & Moore, 1999).

In fact, these referenda often have been passed by substantial margins, despite formal opposition raised by governors or legislatures. Charles Clotfelter and Philip Cook note this trend: "[W]ith remarkable regularity, state governors and legislators have opposed lotteries, only to yield in the end to majority opinion. . . . National polls have recorded steady growth in the approval rating for state lotteries from 48 percent in 1964 to 73 percent in 1982" (Clotfelter & Cook, 1989, p. 236).

While legislators put many gambling proposals on statewide ballots, a sizable number of lotteries and casinos have been proposed via the public initiative process. Initiatives appear to give the public a way to legalize gambling without having to get legislative agreement. They also provide much needed political cover for elected officials. Legislators and governors may be uncomfortable taking the heat in the emotional debate over needed revenue versus the potential social ills of the state owning and operating a lottery. They may feel it politically safer to leave the final decision to the voters.

The ability to hand the question to voters also helps key elected officials such as governors avoid making themselves targets of conservative religious or pro-family groups who would forcefully oppose gambling. One researcher has found that simply the existence of the initiative process in a state makes that state significantly more likely to adopt a lottery than a state where the initiative is unavailable (Boehmke, 1999, p. 15). Lotteries may be more popular with the public than they are with government officials.

Most states that operate lotteries now operate a variety of different games, including instant games, "Lotto," and interstate lotteries such as "Powerball." Several state lotteries also offer keno and video lottery terminals. In those states where they exist, lotteries account for a relatively small percentage of total state revenue, although they have been among the fastest growing revenue sources. In 1996, gross lottery revenues were $16.2 billion, accounting for a small portion of personal expenditures (only a quarter of a percent, as a percent of personal income). Yet, that figure has grown substantially from the $2.1 billion in gross revenues that lotteries brought to the economy in 1982, in which they represented only .0812 percent, as a percent of personal income. Lottery states also collect substantial amounts of privilege tax from the sale of lottery tickets. In 1996, lotteries provided about $13.8 billion to the 37 states where they operate (Christiansen, 1998, p. 41).

Lotteries were among the first state-sponsored forms of gambling throughout the country, and it now appears that familiarity may be breeding acceptance. Table 2.1 shows the year in which each state adopted its lottery, and a careful reading of the table reveals a decidedly regional pattern to the adoption of lotteries. Lotteries first ap-

Table 2.1
Adoptions of the State Lottery

1963	New Hampshire
1967	New York
1970	New Jersey
1972	Connecticut, Massachusetts, Michigan, Pennsylvania
1973	Maryland
1974	Illinois, Maine
1975	Delaware, Ohio, Rhode Island
1978	Vermont
1981	Arizona
1982	Washington
1983	Colorado
1985	California, Iowa, Missouri, Oregon, West Virginia
1986	Florida
1988	Kansas, Montana, South Dakota, Virginia, Wisconsin
1989	Idaho, Indiana, Kentucky, Minnesota
1990	Georgia, Louisiana, Texas
1993	Nebraska
1995	New Mexico
2000	South Carolina

Sources: Clotfelter and Cook, 1989; McGowan, 1994; adoption dates
from election results since 1994.

peared in the late 1960s in the Northeast and soon followed in the West and the Midwest. The regional expansion of lotteries continued throughout the 1970s and early 1980s.

CASINOS

Legal casino gambling began in 1931 in Nevada. The actors involved in the casino policy process, and the beliefs and expectations of these actors, have very much evolved out of the history of the casino industry. The image of casinos was linked for many years to the mob-controlled Las Vegas casinos such as the Flamingo, which was built in 1946 by "Bugsy" Siegel. In 1966, Howard Hughes "was a leading and respected businessman. His entry into Las Vegas and his purchase of several casinos was a watershed event in the transition

Table 2.2
Adoptions of Non-Indian Casinos, Card Rooms, and Gaming Devices

1931	Nevada
1976	New Jersey
1988	California*
1989	Iowa, South Dakota
1990	Colorado
1991	Illinois, Louisiana, Michigan, Mississippi, Missouri
1992	Indiana
1999	Minnesota*

*Allows card rooms only: no blackjack or slot machines are allowed.

Sources: Dombrink & Thompson, 1990; Rose, 2000.

of the Nevada gaming industry" (Dombrink & Thompson, 1990, p. 22). By 1972, major corporate players—including Hilton, Hyatt, and Metro-Goldwyn-Mayer (MGM)—had invested heavily in Nevada and clearly helped to upgrade the image of casinos. Prior to that time, many of the sources of capital for Las Vegas casinos included "questionable" funding such as the Teamsters Central States Pension Fund (Skolnick, 1978).

In 1974, New Jersey attempted to become the second state to allow casino gambling, but the statewide referendum failed to gain the required majority of votes. Two years later, a second, better defined proposal passed. Soon after, some Florida residents sought to make theirs the third casino state. But it was not to be because a referendum to authorize casinos there failed in 1978 (Dombrink & Thompson, 1990).

Nevada and New Jersey held the exclusive on casinos until 1989, when both Iowa and South Dakota passed legislation allowing casino-style gambling. Iowa was the first in modern times to legalize a restricted version of riverboat casino gambling, and by June of that year the area saw the opening of five casino boats on the Mississippi River (Koselka & Palmeri, 1993, p. 71). Since then a number of states—including Colorado, Illinois, Indiana, Louisiana, Michigan, Missouri, and Mississippi,—have legalized various forms of casino gambling. Table 2.2 shows the states that allow casinos, card rooms, and/or gaming devices (typically slot machines) and the dates of adoption.

The spread of casino-style gambling has been much quicker than that of the lotteries or pari-mutuels, as Table 2.2 shows. In less than five years, the number of states allowing some form of casino gaming jumped from just 2 (Nevada and New Jersey) to 22 (Koselka & Palmeri, 1993, p. 70).[1] It is noteworthy that casino gambling has not followed the same regional adoption pattern that lotteries did. Two states in the Deep South—Mississippi and Louisiana—were early adopters of casinos.

Riverboat, resort, and mountain resort casinos are particularly prevalent, but casinos have also been developed in some urban areas including New Orleans, Louisiana, and Detroit, Michigan. There are also more than 300 card clubs operating in the state of California, which are similar to casinos but offer a limited number of games. If Indian gaming is included, some form of casino or card room gambling is now available to residents in 24 states (Rose, 2000).

OVERVIEW OF GAMBLING IN THE UNITED STATES

The spread of gaming may be waning, yet this has to be understood within the context of the extraordinary spread of gambling in the past decade. Statewide elections in 1994, 1995, 1996, 1999, and 2000 resulted in more losses than victories for gambling proponents.

A bid to allow casinos, charity raffles, bingo, and a state lottery in Arkansas failed (65 percent against to 35 percent for) on November 7, 2000; that same day, voters in Maine and West Virginia rejected limited gambling expansion proposals (Rose, 2000). On the November 1996 ballots, there were a total of seven major gambling votes— in Arkansas, Colorado, Iowa, Louisiana, Michigan, Nebraska, and Ohio. Of these votes, only the Michigan one, authorizing the creation of a downtown Detroit casino in an attempt to lure back gamblers who had gone across the river to the new Ontario, Canada, casinos, received enough votes (Nossiter, 1996, p. A9).

In 1999, the South Carolina state legislature shut down 34,000 convenience video poker machines, contingent upon a November 1999 referendum. In October of 2000, the state Supreme Court threw out the referendum but upheld the shutdown, effectively wiping out the existence of the industry in one sweep (Rose, 2000).

As shown in Table 2.3, since 1994, 23 separate ballot initiatives or referenda to legalize various forms of gambling at the state level have

Table 2.3
Results of Statewide Gambling Referenda, 1994–2000

Year	State	Proposed Type	For	Against
1994	Colorado	Slot Machines	8	92
1994	Florida	Casinos	38	62
1994	Minnesota	Video Poker	(defeated)	
1994	Missouri	Slot machines	54	46
1994	New Mexico	Lottery/Video Poker	54	46
1994	Oklahoma	Lottery	(defeated)	
1994	Rhode Island	Casino/Slots	(defeated)	
1994	South Dakota	Slot machines	53	47
1994	Wyoming	Full casinos	31	69
1995	Washington	Indian casinos	33	67
1996	Arkansas	Casinos	39	61
1996	Colorado	New Casinos	32	68
1996	Michigan	Casino in Detroit	52	48
1996	North Dakota	Slot machines	32	68
1996	Ohio	Casinos	38	62
1996	Washington	Indian slots	40	60
1997	California	Indian casinos	(passed)	
1999	Alabama	Lottery	45	55
2000	Arkansas	Casino+lottery	35	65
2000	California	Indian casinos	(passed)	
2000	Maine	Video Lottery	(defeated)	
2000	South Dakota	Raise bet limits	52	48
2000	West Virginia	Limited casino	(defeated)	

Note: Defeated proposals are in bold.

Sources: "Gambling Under Attack," 1996; Rose, 2000.

failed. Gambling scholar William Eadington says that gambling industry fortunes always rise in a poor economy and slump during a booming one (cited in "Gambling Under Attack," 1996, p. 773). That, he contends, at least partially explains why the industry has expanded its operations since 1995 within only a limited range of states.

The gambling industry has taken note of the losses. It has also noted the various attempts to discredit and eliminate its position in public policy, and it has fought back hard. The American Gaming

Association (AGA), an industry lobbying group, was formed in 1994 to fight what it viewed as an onslaught of negative and misleading information.

The AGA lineup of lobbyists reads like a who's who among the political elites of both parties. Among those listed in 1996 were Frank Farenkopf, Jr. (former Republican National Committee chair), Dennis Eckart (former Ohio Democratic congressman), Charles L. Kinney (former chief floor counsel to then-Senate Majority Leader George Mitchell), and Charles Black, who served as an advisor in both the Reagan and Bush administrations (White, 1996).

The AGA now sponsors research, promotes community involvement among its members, and expends considerable time and money in providing information on what it perceives as the benefits of legal gambling for the United States. The industry has also massed significant resources in the political arena. For example, in the 1996 federal elections, gambling interests gave almost $4 million in soft money contributions to the two major political parties (Common Cause, 1997). Party contributions were split nearly evenly between the Democrats and the Republicans.

During the same election cycle, the study shows that union-affiliated gaming employee political action committees (PACs) favored Democrats over Republicans nine-to-one in their direct contributions, but other gaming industry PACs again split their campaign donations evenly between the two parties. Some within the Republican Party have expressed serious concerns about the influx of gambling donations. In November 1997, for instance, Senate Majority Leader Trent Lott (R–MS) was flown to Las Vegas in a jet owned by then-president of Mirage Resorts Steven Wynn for a million dollar fund-raising event for the National Republican Senatorial Committee. Six months later, Senator John Ashcroft (R–MO) blasted the casino industry and said gambling was a cancer on the soul of the country at a public speech before a Biloxi, Mississippi, conference.

According to William Kristol, editor of the conservative magazine, *The Weekly Standard*, "I think [gambling] is one of the issues that highlight[s] the differences between libertarians and business interests in the GOP and social conservatives," within the Republican ranks (quoted in Stone, 1998, p. 1290).

Much of the political influence of gambling is felt at the state level, where key votes on gambling occur every year. One researcher showed gambling industry expenditures in excess of $100 million on various state lobbying efforts between 1990 and 1996 (Koughan, 1997).

The dramatic increase in the political profile of gambling is directly related to the industry's growth in recent years. Overall, the availability of gambling is extensive; several states in the Northeast, Midwest, and West offer all three major forms of gambling. As of 2001, only the states of Alaska, Hawaii, and Utah offer no legal gambling for non-charitable purposes.

THE FEDERAL GOVERNMENT AND LEGAL GAMBLING

The federal government of the United States has never played a major role in the regulation of gambling activity; the vast majority of legal gambling activity in the United States falls under state, and sometimes local, jurisdiction. Clearly, gambling is among the various morality policies placed within the state's jurisdiction by the police powers under the 10th Amendment to the U.S. Constitution.

While some say the federal government could, or should take a greater role in gambling regulation,[2] there are significant questions as to the constitutionality of any federal attempt to impose major new restrictions on gambling. Much depends on the technical legal framework in which one views gambling: Is it morality or is it commerce? Of course, gambling encompasses both concerns. It is quite clear that Congress has the firmly established authority to regulate most commerce. As early as 1824, the Supreme Court in *Gibbons v. Ogden* (22 U.S. 1) declared an expansive view of the Interstate Commerce Clause of the U.S. Constitution: "This power, like all others vested in Congress, is complete in itself, may be exercised to its utmost extent, and acknowledges no limitations, other than are prescribed in the constitution."

It is also clear that the states are considered primary in the regulation of activity deemed to be of a "moral" nature. Notable exceptions to this general rule include the infamous federal attempt at alcohol prohibition and the current federal prohibitions on the use of illegal drugs.[3] Far more examples of state authority over morality policies abound: from marriage and divorce laws to pornography and obscenity regulations to the rare cases such as Nevada where various forms of prostitution have been made legal. Overall, a far greater number of these examples show states taking the lead in morality regulations.

Even so, the federal government's general regulatory authority in the areas of taxation, interstate commerce, criminality, communications, and Indian affairs has created numerous opportunities for congressional, agency, and federal court actions in the area of gambling regulation. For example, when the National Gambling Impact Study Commission released its final report, it included a document listing all current federal regulations applicable to gambling or gaming. That document contains over 800 pages of federal statutes (National Gambling Impact Study Commission [NGISC], 1999). The commission was created by Congress in 1996 and was the third such national panel to be created by Congress in the past 60 years.

A search of Supreme Court cases involving some form of gambling, or relating to a gambling enterprise, has turned up 15 cases, dating back as far as the early 1800s. In 1850, for example, in *Phalen v. Virginia* (49 U.S.163), the Court expressed contempt for lotteries, calling them a form of "widespread pestilence." The *Champion v. Ames* (188 U.S.321) case, often referred to simply as "the lottery case," established in 1903 the Court's intention not to fully cede such cases to state courts, nor to relegate them exclusively to the area of "morality." The federal government continues to play an important, albeit secondary, role in gambling regulation.

The remainder of this chapter considers federal taxation of gambling winnings and losses, regulations pertaining to gambling devices, regulations pertaining to gambling locales, and regulations pertaining to gambling advertising. A brief discussion of the regulation of Indian gaming is included within the section on gambling locales. Nearly all of this material is developed from the NGISC federal legislation data set.

Next, the federal courts' role in enhancing the ability of the federal government to place its imprimatur on various forms of gambling is examined. Finally, the chapter addresses the 1999 NGISC's report, provides a history of the commission's activities, and reviews the findings.

Federal Tax Laws

It is widely accepted that the U.S. tax code is cumbersome, at times ambiguous, and in most aspects rife with exceptions and exemptions.

The tax laws pertaining to wins and losses from gambling are no exception to that general rule. Part of the difficulty stems from the frequently conflicting motives at work in the creation of federal tax laws pertaining to gambling.

Early federal tax statutes were aimed primarily at controlling illegal gambling activities. A 1941 law—the Federal Stamp Tax on coin-operated amusement devices—included a provision to apply the tax to gambling machines. Two similar laws—the Wagering Excise Tax and the Occupational Stamp Tax—were aimed directly at sports, numbers, and horse bookmaking operations (Schmidt, Barr, & Swanson, 1997). Portions of these acts were later ruled unconstitutional, and the Federal Stamp Tax was repealed in 1978.

In a very real sense the modern federal income tax laws continue to seek the same objectives as the earlier laws: to limit gambling activity. Gambling winnings are taxed as ordinary income, and losses are deductible only to the extent of offsetting winnings.

To illustrate, one would measure winnings on a particular wager by using the net gain on the wager. For example, if a $20 bet at the racetrack turns into a $100 win, the net win is $80. If the gambler later loses $50 at a slot machine, however, she cannot simply offset this amount against her $80 win.

Losses must be tracked separately. They are deductible, but only as itemized deductions; thus, gambling losses are not deductible unless the taxpayer itemizes. For those who do itemize, gambling losses are fully deductible and aren't subject to either the 2 percent of adjusted gross income (AGI) "floor," or the 3 percent/80 percent phase out of certain itemized deductions. A second important limitation is that gambling losses are only deductible up to the amount of actual gambling winnings. That is, for tax purposes, losses can be used to "wipe out" gambling income. A taxpayer can never show a net gambling tax loss.

In recognition of the increased prominence of all forms of legal gambling in the U.S. economy, some federal lawmakers have sought to create new federal gambling taxes for the purpose of generating significant new revenues. In 1994, President Bill Clinton proposed a gross gaming revenue tax, similar to the taxes charged by states, on casinos and other gaming sites. The law would have excluded state lotteries and Indian gaming.

The casino and pari-mutuel industries fought back hard, as did most states that already allow, and generate significant tax revenues from, these forms of gambling. The NGISC, created by Congress shortly after this proposal surfaced, did not specifically address the Clinton proposal. After the commission released its report, however, Representative Frank Wolf, a Virginia Republican who sponsored the law creating the commission and outlining its task, said in a June 18, 1999, television interview that he planned to introduce bills to propose a 1 percent federal tax on gross gambling revenues. The proposal also included language prohibiting the ability of gamblers who itemize tax deductions to write off gambling losses against their winnings. This would resurrect an idea floated the prior year by former Senator Dan Coats (R–IN) who estimated that it would generate $1.1 billion over four years. Coats withdrew his original proposal after it met opposition from Senate leaders (Stone, 1998).

A flurry of activity followed the Wolf announcement, and within hours the legislative delegation from Nevada, as well as lobbyists from the AGA, had met with leaders of both Houses of Congress. Dick Armey (R–TX) who served as House Majority Leader, quickly released a statement opposing any federal taxes on the gambling industry (Batt, 1999).

Regulating Gambling Devices and Activities

Much of the federal government's role in the regulation of gambling in the United States has occurred in the area of regulating the devices and paraphernalia associated with it. One of the first major pieces of such legislation was passed by Congress in the late 1940s. Section 1301 of the Federal Code prohibits the importation or transportation of illegal lottery tickets, either on one's person or via third-party carriers such as express delivery services.

Congress passed similar antigambling laws regarding casino devices beginning in 1951. The Gaming Devices Transportation Act was one in a series of laws passed during a period of intense scrutiny over illegal gambling that was carried out in various locations. These laws make it a federal crime to transport gambling devices such as slot machines into states where such machines are not legal and authorized by the state. Some of these laws also specify jurisdictional concerns and require the registration of all gambling device manufacturers and dealers. Changes that are more recent allow for the forfeiture of any illegal machines confiscated by federal authorities (15 USC Sec. 1171).

Much of the impetus for these laws came from public hearings conducted by Senator Estes Kefauver (D–TN) during the 1950s. The Mississippi Gulf Coast was one of several sites targeted by the senator's team of investigators. The Mississippi situation came to the fore when Kefauver brought his committee to the Biloxi, Mississippi, post office for 12 hours of testimony on October 22, 1951 (Palermo, 1998).

The hearing was the culmination of a three-week undercover operation that began when Kefauver was tipped off that Mississippi clubs were subscribing to a horse-race wire service provided by Continental Press in Chicago and Daily Sports News out of New Orleans. Both organizations were thought to have ties to the Carlos Marchello crime syndicate, already under investigation by Kefauver. Among the committee members attending the hearings on the coast was Senator Lester Hunt (D–WY), an Armed Services Committee member who relied heavily on information gathered for that committee by officials at the nearby Keesler Air Force Base.

Keesler officials conducted a survey of Harrison County, Mississippi, businesses and found that some 327 bars, supper clubs, and establishments were offering illegal gambling and illegal liquor, and that much of it was made available to airmen. Keesler officials also counted some 1,275 slot machines in business establishments ranging from restaurants to saloons to hotels and even in the Greyhound bus station. All told, they found 72 blackjack tables, 55 poker tables, 31 dice tables, 10 roulette wheels, and 11 horse-race wires—all of them illegal under Mississippi state law (Palermo, 1998).

Eventually, the entire investigation was turned over to then-Senator Lyndon Johnson (D–TX), who chaired the Senate's Armed Services Committee. Kefauver told Johnson that the illegal gambling was eating up $500,000 of the air base's $4 million monthly payroll. Testimony before the Organized Crime Committee also included stories about pilots pawning their uniforms in order to get cash for illegal gambling. Kefauver also told the committee that two service members had reportedly committed suicide because of their enormous gambling debts (Palermo, 1998).

The Kefauver commission concentrated on illegal gambling activities in Illinois and Louisiana and on ties between legal and illegal gambling in Nevada as well. Concerns over the impact of organized crime were addressed, in part, in the nation's racketeering laws. Illegal gambling businesses are specifically included among the "unlawful activities" listed as part of the racketeering statutes. For purposes of the racketeering laws, gambling is described as "any business enterprise involving gambling . . . in violation of the laws of the State in which they are committed or of the United States" (96 USC Sect. 1961). The Organized Crime Control Act of 1970 also includes several prohibitions on illegal bookmaking and organized numbers games that often have been run by the mob (15 USC Sect. 1177).

The Federal Code includes prohibitions on the use of the postal system to facilitate gambling. Mailing lottery tickets, bookmaking information, and similar materials is a federal crime punishable by fines and possible jail time (18 USC Sect. 1301 and 1302). Congress has also tried to eliminate true "gambling" activities from within the nation's commodities markets (a task admittedly fraught with difficulties). In language as clear as it could possibly muster, Congress has tried to assert that persons who gamble on the markets or in association with them will be punished (42 USC Sect. 12211).

This language has recently come under scrutiny as the practice of "day-trading" has grown from a fringe hobby into a more respectable "career." Firms have sprung up that offer training and/or provide facilities for day-traders. Some in Congress believe these activities may be illegal under the existing antigambling laws. Day-trading firms are, according to Senator Carl Levin (D–MI) "turning the most trusted market in the world into a virtual gambling casino. We have to pay attention to this new and growing phenomenon so we don't wake up one morning and sift through the debris of a broken economy" (Statement of Senator Carol Levin, 1999).

The federal government targets other gambling situations, clearly illegal under existing law. Federal laws provide for deportation and/or denial of immigration to noncitizens who engage in illegal gambling or to those for whom gambling is the principal source of income (42 USC Sect. 3796).

Money laundering is another illegal activity with historic ties to gambling. The 1970 Bank Secrecy Act did not originally address money laundering through casinos, but changes made in 1985 added casinos to the list of "financial institutions" required to report financial transactions of $10,000 or more. The law has faced several legal challenges but was upheld by the Supreme Court in 1974 in *California Banker's Association v. Schultz* (416 U.S. 21).

Recent attempts to curtail gambling under federal law include proposed bans on Internet gambling, and a law to make betting on all college sporting events illegal. The 1992 Professional and Amateur Sports Protection Act (28 USC Sect. 3702) forbids wagering on competitive sporting events such as college or professional sports, and forbids state and local governments from authorizing such activities, but it included a grandfather clause allowing states where such activities were then legal to continue offering sports betting. The proposed law (S. 2021 and H.R. 3575 of 1999–2000) would repeal the exceptions. Not surprisingly, legal sports book operators in Nevada have amassed tremendous resources in opposition to these bills.

Regulations Pertaining to Gambling Locales

Congress, through its Interstate Commerce Clause powers, has also forbidden gambling in certain places and situations outright. For example, transportation regulations covering airlines prohibit the use of any form of gambling device on board aircraft used in international flights (49 USC Sect. 41311). Additional regulations stipulate the circumstances under which gambling may take place on board cruise ships and other vessels bound for international waters (26 USC Sect. 527). Generally, ships must be underway, not docked. A 1996 estimate of the total amounts wagered on regular deepwater cruises was about $200 million, but wagers on "cruises to nowhere" (e.g., those cruises specifically operated as a short pleasure trip, often providing opportunities for gambling, dining, and/or entertainment) was $5.5 billion (Christiansen, 1998).

Title 25 of the U.S. Code pertains to federal relations with Indian tribes and contains those sections of federal law allowing casinos on Indian lands. The 1988 Indian Gaming Regulatory Act (25 USC Sect. 2701) enables tribes to operate gaming on reservation property if the form of gambling is already legal in the state in which the reservation is located. The forms of gambling are divided into classes; it is Class III gambling (casinos, slot machines, and pari-mutuels of various kinds) that has become particularly prevalent.

Under the law, tribes may seek a compact to operate Class III gaming *of any kind* if *any other kind* of Class III gaming is legal within that state. Thus, for example, states with legal horse- or dog-racing tracks may become subject to the provisions when a tribe wishes to open a casino. Kelly describes how "[a] clever tribal attorney convinced a federal judge (*Lac du Flambeau Indians v. State of Wisconsin*) that since Wisconsin had a state lottery and since the lottery consisted of prize, chance, and consideration, and since all casinos had games consisting of prize, chance, and consideration, therefore Wisconsin had to negotiate a compact with the tribes which would allow Indian casinos" (1997, p. 216).

Tribes must negotiate a compact with state officials, and several states have asserted that Congress overstepped the bounds of the 10th Amendment when it created a requirement that state governments enter into these negotiations with tribes. Thus far, however, the Supreme Court has upheld the 1988 law.[4]

While much has been written regarding the legal maneuvering of various tribes seeking compacts with states that would allow them to operate casinos or other gambling venues,[5] relatively little has been written about the actions of the Bureau of Indian Affairs in the negotiations. The bureau has exhibited a tendency to serve the tribal governments' interests in these negotiations with state governments, prompting officials in several states to cry "foul."

Representative Frank Wolf (R–VA) raised one area of concern. Following tribal recognition by the Bureau of Indian Affairs, a Connecticut-area tribe began seeking a gaming compact with the state. Wolf and several other gambling opponents questioned the lax methods used by the bureau to authenticate the group's claims to tribal rights.[6] He has called on the U.S. Government Accounting Office (GAO) to oversee the process and for stricter requirements for tribal recognition, in light of the desire of many tribes to open gaming facilities.

Others feel that the Bureau should take a greater role in oversight of Indian gaming. Proponents often voice their concern that the bureau should be able to show why Indian gaming has been a success. For example, Senator Tom Daschle (D–SD) in a hearing on gaming's impact on Native Americans raised concern over the Bureau's lack of research into economic growth, job creation, and related impact issues. "I am puzzled as to why you couldn't provide that," he told Bureau representatives (Kelly, 1997, p. 226).

Regulations Pertaining to Gambling Advertising

The Federal Communications Commission (FCC) has been given authority to regulate advertising on the nation's television and radio stations, yet Congress has chosen to make advertising gambling a part of the criminal code. Within the pertinent sections of the criminal code are several subsections pertaining specifically to advertisements for gambling establishments. The passages originally applied both to casino operations and to lotteries.

As state governments began to enact lotteries in an effort to generate revenues, the state lottery agencies began to seek an exemption from the criminal prohibition. Congress' response was to provide the exemption, but only for broadcasters in the same state where the lottery was located (18 USC Sect. 1304). The IGRA provides specific exemptions from Section 1304 for Indian casinos. A specific piece of legislation passed in 1988, the Charity Games Advertising Clarification Act (18 USC Sect. 1307), also exempts certain state-run and charitable casino games from the advertising bans—and extends those exemptions even to advertisements carried by stations in states where such activity is not legal.

The impact of these advertising bans, and the subsequent numerous and varied exemptions to them, has been to give the FCC (which effectively handles all cases of violations for the Solicitor General) broad power to decide what is, and is not, a legal advertisement for gambling. As of the end of the 1990s, the general rule in effect was to allow ads for state lotteries, but only in states where lotteries were legal; casino amenities and casino brand names in any state (e.g., casinos could advertise about their food, entertainment, and ambience, but not specifically mention their gambling activities); and Indian gambling in any state. The situation was ripe for Court action, and the courts were happy to oblige.

The Federal Courts' Role

The Supreme Court in 1999 made a dramatic change in federal public policies relating to gambling when it announced its ruling in *Greater New Orleans Broadcasting Association v. United States* (*GNOBA vs. U.S.* ([387 U.S. 98, 1999]). The 1999 decision decries the patchwork nature of federal regulations pertaining to gambling advertisements. It scolds Congress for the incoherence of its policies and declares that the existing regulations, as applied, arbitrarily condone some ads while prohibiting others of a very similar nature. "The federal government's regulations," said the Court, "neither reasonably promote important social goals nor accommodate competing

State and private interests. All told," the Court added, "the FCC's policies regarding gambling advertising violate First Amendment protections of commercial speech" (*GNOBA v. U.S.*).

This was by no means the first time the U.S. Supreme Court had been asked to resolve disputes about gambling. Early case law, most of it from the 1950s, followed a flurry of federal activity aimed at eradicating illegal gambling, spurred by the actions of Senator Estes Kefauver and others. In *United States v. Korpan* (354 U.S. 271, 1957), the Supreme Court held that any coin-operated device that paid cash prizes was subject to the provisions of 26 USC, Sect. 4461, and a $25 per unit tax on gambling machines. The Court said the federal government had gone too far, however, when it required every manufacturer or dealer of gambling devices to meet certain reporting requirements or risk forfeiture of those devices even in cases in which interstate commerce was not appreciably affected (*United States v. Five Gambling Devices Etc.*, [346 U.S. 441, 1953]).

The Court heard few gambling-related cases during the 1970s and 1980s. When the issue again arose, it did so in the form of Indian gaming. In 1987, the Court ruled that California had no legal authority to prohibit Indian tribes there to open and operate bingo halls or casinos, since other similar forms of gambling are allowable under California law (*California v. Cabazon Band of Mission Indians* [480 U.S. 202, 1987]).

Congress followed the decision by passing the Indian Gaming Regulatory Act in 1988 but controversies continued. The new law not only required states allowing gambling to enter into compacts with Indian tribes, but it also provided an avenue for tribes to sue, in federal court, states that refused to do so. The Seminole tribe in Florida did just that when, in 1991, the state refused to enter into compact negotiations. The Supreme Court said that Congress overstepped its boundaries in authorizing the lawsuits, since states are constitutionally protected from lawsuits by sovereign immunity (*Seminole Tribe of Florida v. Florida* [116 S.Ct. 1144, 1996]).

CONGRESSIONALLY FUNDED STUDIES OF GAMBLING

When Congress decided in 1973 to fund a study of the impacts of the legal gambling industry on the United States, there was no Indian gaming, only a small handful of states had lotteries, casinos were legal only in Nevada, and pari-mutuel wagering at horse and dog tracks (then legal in more than two dozen states) was the prime area of concern. In 1996 Congress decided to fund another gambling impacts study. This time, the tracks were in a serious slump, but either a state lottery or some form of casino was available in nearly every U.S. state.

The Commission on the Review of the National Policy Toward Gambling was established in 1973 and published its final report in 1976. Under the title *Gambling in America*, it detailed the extent and availability of gambling, included survey-based profiles of gamblers, and concluded that most Americans felt legal gambling should be made available to those persons who want it ("Gambling in America," 1976).

The National Gambling Impact Study Commission was formed in 1996 following a tremendous lobbying effort by antigambling forces. Thomas Grey, of the National Coalition Against Legalized Gambling, worked alongside several other religious groups—who opposed the rapid spread of casinos in the early 1990s—to push for a comprehensive study of the industry and its effects on the American economy, society, and psyche. Representative Frank Wolf (R–VA) sponsored the authorizing legislation.

The law allowed Democratic President Bill Clinton, Republican House Speaker Newt Gingrich, and Republican Senate Majority Leader Trent Lott jointly to appoint a nine-member panel to design and oversee the study, and to author the final report. Lobbyists on both sides of the issue pressed hard to have representatives of their position on the panel.

The panel that emerged was split evenly between gambling supporters and opponents. It consisted of conservative Christian activists and gambling industry executives, plus additional members from a variety of backgrounds. The membership roster included well-known family values activist and chairwoman Kay James, Focus on the Family President Dr. James Dobson, MGM Grand Chair Terrence Lanni, and six others with equally diverse views on gambling.[7]

The law also gave the commission a budget of $4 million, along with the subpoena power it needed to gain access to various state and industry reports and other documents. The panel was not given the power to subpoena individuals to testify, however. The commission had to complete its work under a congressionally imposed deadline of no longer than two years.

Once the entire panel had been selected, the group began to map a plan for completion of the enormous task. A small number of commission staff members were selected and hired. Small portions of the needed research were to be done in-house, but the majority of the research would have to be contracted to companies, universities, or individuals that possessed the necessary skills and experience.

Early on, the commission's members decided that they needed substantial public input in addition to the various research reports they had authorized. A series of public hearings was scheduled during 1997 and 1998. Dozens of individuals, ranging from industry executives to pathological gamblers, from police officers to gambling regulators, spoke before the commission at hearings in ten different cities. Some cited statistics. Others told personal stories. A few speakers wept openly. In the end, supporters and opponents of gambling used the collected testimony of the various speakers primarily as a weapon: few direct comments or details from these hearings ended up in the final report.

The formal research, on the other hand, provided the bulk of material for the final document, which is now a rich, public repository of information about gambling, gamblers, and their impacts. A massive national survey by the NORC, detailed analyses of several dozen state, local, and industry studies of gambling, comprehensive statistical models of aggregate economic and social impact data, studies of state and federal legislation and regulation pertaining to gambling, and a comprehensive review of Indian gaming were all included.

The final report of the commission was made public in June 1999. Weighing in at over 200 pages, the report chronicled the development of gambling into a more than $50 billion per year industry, while also demonstrating the sometimes devastating personal and community impacts wrought by gambling addictions and related social ills. The document included an exhaustive list of 76 separate recommendations. Only one of the 76 recommended steps (a moratorium on further gambling expansion) could be taken without changes to existing federal or state laws.

Among the recommendations were a few surprises and many items that were long anticipated. The commission recommended, for example, that state governments should take steps to end "convenience gambling" and hold off on any new gambling authorizations while the overall impacts of gambling continue to be studied. The group called for new laws to curb political donations from gambling industry groups or firms, and challenged states to conduct their own on-going research before allowing any new gambling establishments to open. The report also scolded state lottery agencies and implored them to self-police their lottery advertising practices.

The federal government was targeted in several of the commission's recommendations as well. The report called for a 1 percent federal tax on gambling proceeds, as described earlier in this chapter. Betting on all college sporting activities should be federally banned, and Congress should enact sanctions on Internet gambling while simultaneously removing protection for the industry through the nation's credit laws. The report also called for federal laws requiring "cooling-off periods" between service in gaming regulatory bodies and employment within the gambling industry.

Other recommendations include clarification of language about the various "classes" of gambling in IGRA, the removal of ATMs from betting areas at casinos and racetracks, and the imposition of a nationwide 21-year-old legal gambling age restriction. The report also included calls for laws requiring "warning signs" about the dangers and risks of gambling at gambling venues, and for Indian tribes to use some of their gaming windfall to create non-gaming economic opportunities for their citizens in order to reduce their overall dependence on gambling revenues (NGISC, 1999).

The release of the report to Congress, the White House, and the various state and tribal governments that operate legal gambling resulted in a flurry of press coverage and the introduction of a small number of federal and state bills. Representative Wolf introduced legislation to create a federal gaming tax and to ban sports betting, and Senator John Kyl (R–AZ) sponsored a ban on Internet casinos and sports books.

Representative Wolf managed to convince the GAO to conduct a review of the NGISC methodology and findings and to conduct an independent study of the economic and social impacts of casinos on Atlantic City. The findings, released in April 2000, generally confirm and replicate the NGISC's final report. In it, the GAO states that it could find "no conclusive evidence on whether or not gambling caused increased social problems in Atlantic City," since available statistical data sources and tracking systems "do not collect data on the causes of these incidents" and thus they cannot accurately be linked to gambling (GAO, 2000).

However, the NGISC's recommendations have largely gone unheeded, in part because the gambling industry's growth had already slowed considerably by the time the report was released. Since it was made public, Michigan has begun operations in its first Detroit casino; Mississippi, New Jersey, and Nevada continue to take applications for new licensees; and California has begun the process of reviewing literally hundreds of applications for Indian casinos.

South Carolina successfully repealed its convenience gambling by eliminating video poker, although its citizens voted for a new state lottery; and Alabama, as discussed earlier, defeated a lottery referendum. A few statewide studies of the impacts of gambling have been funded, and both the National Science Foundation and the National Institutes of Health have called for gambling-related research applications.

Overall, the gambling industry continues a steady pattern of growth in the United States, and it is that growth that is responsible for the lackluster reception that the NGISC's report received. Politically, the gambling industry has proved it is a force to be reckoned with because it possesses the resources needed to amass huge campaigns for passage of gambling and to continually lobby government for favorable legislation.

Clearly, gambling policy has involved a defined set of actors: legislators and governors, voters, and gambling industry representatives, along with occasional input from federal legislators. The expectations they bring appear to be shaped to some extent by the history of gambling in the United States and also, perhaps, by their own moral views of gambling. The development of gambling policy has been incremental, even piecemeal, and has progressed for the most part without significant rational consideration of the longer-term impacts for the states and localities in which it occurs.

This chapter also highlights some of the key political differences between lotteries and casino gambling. Lotteries are state-owned, and have been created almost exclusively as a mechanism for generating state revenues. There was a substantial growth in both the number and scope of lotteries in response to concerns over potential economic downturns and increasing pressures from industry lobbying groups (Wohlenberg, 1992). As federal programs devolved to state governments, these governments were forced to find new revenues to pay for them.

Likewise, state and local economic development policies took a major hit during the 1980s and into the 1990s, with the continued consolidation and pullback of various federal programs (Thompson & Gazel, 1997). A recession during the late 1980s and early 1990s further stimulated a desire to find new ways to promote state and local economic development. Casinos became a popular new solution. While in some instances the process of allowing casinos may have followed a similar course to that used by lotteries, the goals and political situations surrounding casino adoptions were very different.

Significant information about the morality policy process is still missing. Much information about the goals and strategies employed by various participants in the process can be obtained through examination of specific instances of gambling campaigns, and that is the focus of the next chapter.

NOTES

1. An interesting aspect of the growth in legalized gambling is the legalization of tribal gambling operations on Native American reservations. Since the passage of the Indian Gaming Regulatory Act in 1988, 45 Native American tribes have signed compacts with 13 states to permit Class III gambling operations (which includes casinos, pari-mutuels, and lotteries) on their reservations (McCullough, 1992, p. 1)

2. Robert Goodman is one vocal critic who has argued for increased federal regulation of gambling. See his book *The Luck Business* (1995).

3. Kenneth Meier (1994) presents a thorough accounting of both federal and state efforts at regulating the sale and use of alcohol and drugs.

4. See, for example, *Seminole Tribe of Florida v. Florida, 1994* (116 S.Ct. 114) and *California v. Cabazon Band of Mission Indians, 1987* (480 U.S. 202).

5. A fascinating study of the interplay between Indian gaming authorization and issues of native sovereignty is Thompson and Dever's 1997 article.

6. Representative Wolf's congressional website (available at http://www.house.gov/wolf) includes the full history of these actions.

7. The additional members were Robert Loescher, William Bible, Richard Leone, Leo McCarthy, Dr. Paul Moore, and John Wilhelm.

3

The Politics of
Gambling Adoptions

Various forms of gambling have been adopted by state governments in the United States primarily as a means of raising revenue. What has rarely been considered, though, is how states decide whether to adopt legal gambling. If elected leaders believe gambling is the right decision for their state, how do they then choose from among the variety of legal gambling forms? This line of questioning ties directly into the morality policy process model and helps to shed light on the strategies and specific benefit expectations of various gambling policy participants.

Once a decision has been reached to adopt a lottery, a casino, or other form of gambling, the state still has many choices to make. How will this new gambling enterprise be established? How will it be regulated? Who will have the authority?

CASE STUDIES OF THE POLITICS OF
GAMBLING ADOPTION

Case studies reveal key points about the questions raised in the morality policy process model. The states to be examined are Colorado, Illinois, Louisiana, and New Jersey,[1] all of which have enacted multiple state gambling policies, and Alabama, which has only adopted pari-mutuel wagering at one horse track and several dog tracks and recently failed in its bid to begin a state lottery.

The states selected for inclusion were chosen based on a variety of factors, including an attempt to represent several different geographic regions, an attempt to include both adopters and non-adopters, an attempt to include both early and later adopters, and the quantity and availability of usable information. The goal is to understand the politics of gambling policy adoptions, so the extent to which these states are, or are not, typical of others is of relatively little concern.

New Jersey: Important Precedents

New Jersey was among the first states to make betting at horse tracks legal shortly after the depression (Joyce, 1979, p. 152). The state legislature adopted pari-mutuel betting in 1939, and the provision was incorporated into the revised state constitution of 1947, along with a stipulation that any new forms of gambling must meet with voter approval (Sternlieb & Hughes, 1983, p. 20).

The early referendum votes are one potential source of information about pre-lottery public sentiment regarding gambling in New Jersey, since earlier statewide public opinion polls on the subject are generally not available. With horse racing already operating in the state, voters adopted amusement games in the 1959 vote by 59 percent, then adopted the state lottery in 1969 by 80 percent, and finally in 1972 overwhelmingly adopted legalized non-charity bingo by better than 85 percent. The public's approval of casinos at the polls was less solid; the first authorization referendum failed in 1974 (Pollock, 1987, p. 13).

New Hampshire and New York were the first states to create their own lotteries, and pressure rose quickly in New Jersey to follow suit. The political success of these early lotteries, coupled with the extent of mobility and cross-state traffic in the region, pushed the New Jersey legislature to propose the lottery in 1969, just five years after New Hampshire's groundbreaking adoption.

Lottery sales went from $78 million in its first year of operation (1971) to $417 million just over a decade later in 1983 (Sternlieb & Hughes, 1983, p. 174). Public interest in the lottery has remained high as shown by the survey research shown in Table 3.1. Lottery play among survey respondents grew from 56 percent playing at least once in 1982 to 76 percent playing at least once in 1988.

Table 3.1
New Jersey Residents' Opinions on Casinos and the Lottery,
1979–1988

"Have you ever played the New Jersey Lottery?"

	Yes	No
1982	56	44
1986	78	21
1988	76	24

"Are you in favor or opposed to legalized casino gambling in Atlantic City?"

	Favor	Oppose	Don't Know
1979	64	30	6
1980	68	26	6
1982	72	22	6
1986	77	14	8

*Source: The Star-Ledger/*Eagleton Poll telephone random samples of 800 New Jersey
residents each. The polls have a sample error of +/−3.5 percent. Information
obtained from press releases dated 8/17/86, 6/2/87, and 2/28/88.

The 1974 campaign for a casino had its roots in much earlier efforts. In 1958, Mildred Fox, president of the Women's Chamber of
Commerce in Atlantic City, proposed the idea as a way to keep the
area's hotels open for a longer season. Illegal gambling was already
common at the resort. "Every little store that had newspapers in the
front had gambling in the back," according to Fox (quoted in Pollock, 1987, p.12). The 1974 referendum was to include other regions
as well, which probably made voting against it that much easier for
state residents. It failed on a 1.2 million to 800,000 vote (Dombrink
& Thompson, 1990, p. 28).

The 1976 vote was entirely different. Through public hearings and
debate, and through the urgings of casino-supporter Governor Bren-
dan Byrne, it was decided that the second referendum would not be
of the open-ended type (allowing casino gambling throughout the
state following local voters' approval); instead, it would only authorize casinos for Atlantic City.

"The state of New Jersey—in the persons of the governor and
influential Atlantic City legislators—gave its blessing to the referendum early and wholeheartedly," according to Dombrink and Thompson (1990, p. 29). Another key factor in changing voters' minds

involved decisions about where casino tax revenues would go (Pollock, 1987, p. 14).

"Remembering that the opposition of church and law enforcement had been most effective among the state's army of elderly citizens," according to Demaris (1986, p. 52) supporters came up with a new plan. Tax revenues derived from casinos would go into a fund to be applied "solely to reduce property taxes, rentals, and telephone, gas, electric, and municipal utilities charges of eligible senior citizens and disabled residents of the state" (Demaris, 1986, p. 52).

This move, in effect, allowed referendum voters to view casinos not in terms of morality and potential crime but in terms of economic self-interest. The ploy was enhanced by the use of billboards, bumper stickers, and commercials with elderly persons in wheelchairs pleading for passage, and everywhere could be seen the slogan: "Help Yourself" (Demaris, 1986, p. 57). The Committee to Rebuild Atlantic City (CRAC) outspent casino opponents two to one, spending four times more than proponents had spent in 1974 (Pollock, 1987, p. 14). Not surprisingly, on the second try, the Atlantic City casino authorization passed with nearly 57 percent of the vote (Joyce, 1979, p. 158). Statewide polls show increases in support for casinos, such as support for lotteries, and as Table 2.5 shows, interest in casinos appears to have grown over time, as well.

The Eagleton Poll in New Brunswick, New Jersey, has frequently asked questions regarding various forms of gambling. For example, in a 1986 survey, respondents were asked whether they think the state raising revenues from taxes on gambling, such as the lottery and the casinos, is a good or a bad idea. Overwhelmingly, as shown in Table 3.2, 70 percent of the respondents felt that this is a good policy.

Other poll questions are also helpful in determining which factors may influence the adoption process. In a 1988 telephone survey of 800 residents, respondents were asked a series of questions that appear to have been designed to get at the underlying reasons for their support or non-support of state gambling policy, based on a series of seven statements. Of the seven statements, four showed that the respondents were nearly evenly split between those saying they agree and those saying they disagree.[2]

Two statements showed the greatest percentage in agreement: (1) People are going to gamble anyway, so there is nothing wrong with the state raising money through the lottery. (2) The lottery is something the state should provide because the people who live here want

Table 3.2
New Jersey Residents' Views on Taxes and the Lottery, 1981–1989

"The state collects tax revenue to support public services from various forms of gambling—such as the Lottery and casinos in Atlantic City. In general, do you think this is a good or a bad way for state government to raise money" (1986).

Good	Bad	Don't Know
70	18	12

"People are going to gamble anyway, so there's nothing wrong with the state raising money through the lottery" (1988).

Agree	Disagree	Don't Know
78	18	4

"The lottery is something the state should provide because the people who live here want it" (1988).

Agree	Disagree	Don't Know
77	19	4

*Source: The Star-Ledger/*Eagleton Poll telephone random samples of 800 New Jersey residents each. The polls have a sample error of +/−3.5 percent. Information obtained from press releases dated 8/17/86, 2/28/88, and 3/19/89.

it. These statements received 78 percent and 77 percent agreement, respectively, from poll respondents. Clearly, as these poll results show, New Jersey residents have developed a comfort level with at least certain forms of gambling.

The gaming industry in Atlantic City at times has had financial difficulties, but today is solid. Still, the industry is not without its troubles. The twentieth anniversary year for gaming in Atlantic City saw the prospect of a gaming tax hike in the state legislature (a move that was eventually defeated). In that same year, the bankrupt Sands Hotel and Casino on the boardwalk received Bankruptcy Court approval for a $13.4 million renovation plan ("What's News," 1998, p. 4).

The Casino Control Commission reports to state residents monthly regarding the status of the earmarked Casino Revenue Fund, into which the 8 percent tax on the "win" (or revenues before taxes and expenses are paid) plus any fines collected in excess of $600,000 must go. That fund earned $309.3 million in fiscal year 1997, plus another

$1.1 million in interest on accrued assets held by the fund. The vast majority of those funds were expended on physical and mental health services for the state's elderly and disabled residents, who are still among the most ardent supporters of gaming in the state (Casino Control Commission, 1999).

New Jersey residents have learned firsthand that the framing of the debate over gambling is crucial to its chances of gaining support. If supporters of a proposed form of gambling focus on the potential revenues and (where applicable) on the area to which those revenues will go, they can often out-poll opponents if they focus on more abstract questions of morality. The New Jersey experience has provided a kind of "laboratory" to which other states considering gambling can turn. In fact, many states have purposefully modeled their legislative actions after the New Jersey successes, and purposefully tried to avoid the several New Jersey failures.

Illinois: Competition Is Critical

Illinois has had various legal forms of pari-mutuel wagering since the middle of the nineteenth century, but its focus on gambling as a source of state revenue has become greatly heightened since a 1989 decision in neighboring Iowa to allow casino-style gambling aboard riverboats. Illinois' state lottery, in operation since 1974, was among the earliest, and most successful, state lottery systems in the nation (Clotfelter & Cook, 1989, p. 221). Illinois' pari-mutuel industry is also one of the healthier in what generally has been a depressed gaming sector.

Illinois, like all states, is engaged in intense interstate competition. That competition occurs along the lines of industry, education, tourism, and politics. The state must compete with its prosperous neighbors in the Midwest for jobs, population, and growth. Chicago, the state's largest city, also competes head to head with major tourist, political, and industrial cities such as New York City, the Washington D.C. metro area, and Boston. All of this has figured prominently into the various gambling debates that have occurred in Illinois.

For example, in 1972 and 1973, when the state lottery was first debated, its backers asserted that tourists coming to New York, New Jersey, and other states liked having the opportunity to play the lotteries in those states. It was their contention that Illinois needed a lottery to remain competitive ("Lottery Backers," 1973, p. A5.) By the mid-1980s, Illinois lottery sales, which had been growing at a rate of about 30 percent annually, suddenly began to skid to about 3 percent growth. In order to boost sales and remain competitive, advertising budgets were increased and marketing efforts were intensified (Calonius, 1991, p. 112).

The state's pari-mutuel facilities also increased their ad budgets in the early 1990s, partly in response to stepped up marketing by neighboring Indiana (Calonius, 1991, p. 112). When Governor James "Big Jim" Thompson proposed riverboat casinos in 1990, he mentioned the newly operating riverboats in Iowa, and a plan was crafted to give the troubled tracks a portion of riverboat casino revenues, thus effectively buying their support. The governor successfully shepherded the casinos through the state legislature as a form of "economic development for depressed local economies as well as [a way to provide] a new source of revenue for local units of government" (Truitt, 1997, p. 132).

In signing the legislation, the Republican governor noted that the new Illinois casinos would allow higher stakes, and thus be able to draw gamblers away from Iowa (Baker, 1990, p. 22). Democrats, particularly those in the Chicago area, were generally opposed to casinos, but Thompson was able to gain passage of the law by specifically limiting riverboats to areas with a population of no more than 3 million. The act provided for only ten licenses (Truitt, 1997, p. 135).

As the casinos' success increased, calls soon began to drop the exclusion of Chicago and Cook County from casino licensing. Chicago Mayor Richard Daley, approached in March of 1992 by a consortium of hotel and casino management companies, proposed a $2 billion complex to include casinos, slot machines, and other forms of entertainment similar to that found in Atlantic City and Las Vegas. In a statewide poll conducted by the *Chicago Tribune*, the strongest opposition to the Chicago casino was from the northern half of the state, an area where riverboat casinos were doing well. Overall, 48 percent of the poll's 700 respondents opposed the Chicago casino, whereas 32 percent favored it (cited in Reardon, 1993, p. 2C).

Governor Thompson and a lobbying group of riverboat operators vowed to fight the Chicago land-based casino just days after the poll results were made public ("Thompson Vows," 1992, p. 1D). Another poll conducted by a private firm on behalf of the proposed-casino's operators found that when expected revenues and job growth from the casino were explained to poll participants, overall support of a Chicago casino increased to 65 percent (Reardon, 1993, p. 7C). A story in the May 30, 1993 *Chicago Tribune* quoted poll results showing that support for a Chicago casino had increased substantially. That increase was especially noticeable when proposals included some version of a combination casino/theme park to enhance the casino's attractiveness for tourists ("State's Mood," 1993, p. 6A).

Under Governor Jim Edgar, the downtown casino idea ultimately died, yet Chicago visitors and residents still have several area casinos, including the Empress in Joliet, the Grand Victoria in Elgin, and the Hollywood in Aurora. Interestingly, Edgar proposed increasing the level of taxation on the largest casinos to boost revenues for schools, but the casino industry fought it heavily. As recently as mid-2000, controversy continued to brew over a proposed riverboat in the Chicago suburb of Rosemont. The site was ultimately given the go-ahead to build a "boat-in-a-moat" (Rose, 2000). The selected area is filled with hotels and convention halls and sandwiched between O'Hare International Airport and the city of Chicago; it is considered by financial experts to be the most lucrative casino site in the state ("Frustration Builds," 2000).

Internal competition does not appear to be hurting existing gambling either; the lottery recorded its second highest sales figure in 1995, three years after casinos were allowed ("Riverboats Haven't Sunk," 1995, p. C2). Late in 1997, the state legislature passed a revision to the riverboat casino tax, which shifted from a flat 20 percent rate to a progressive tax with marginal rates as high as 35 percent. This action increased the level of competition for casino players, especially in light of the expanded number of boats operating in nearby Indiana.

Gross casino revenues for Illinois appeared to have peaked in 1995 at $1.2 billion, falling to only $1.1 billion in 1997 ("Gaming Faces Challenges," 1998, p. 1). In light of the declines, gaming industry representatives successfully lobbied the state legislature for a relaxation of cruising regulations and other limitations to make them more competitive.

The debate in Illinois suggests that some measure of the level of competition, such as the presence of gambling in neighboring states, can play an important role in the shaping of gambling policy. The Illinois gambling policy adoptions also suggest that competition within the state among various forms of gambling may play a role in decisions about additional forms; pari-mutuel facilities may need to be brought on board for casino proposals to succeed. Furthermore, the potential to generate new revenues for the state is a key factor in that competitive scheme. Governor Tommy Thompson, a long-time opponent of expanding gambling in Illinois, was reported late in 2000 to have cut a secret deal with the Menominee tribe that opens the door for a massive casino in Kenosha. Details have become available slowly; the state will reportedly get at least $20 million annually ("Thompson Cuts," 1999).

Colorado: Reviving the Wild West

In many ways, Colorado is typical of other states that have experienced an expansion of legal gambling. The state had its own colorful history of illegal and quasi-legal gambling, going as far back as the times of westward expansion and the great Gold Rush of the 1800s. Betting on horse races, poker games, and similar activities were widespread. Blevins and Jensen (1998) detailed the early history of gambling in the mining towns of Deadwood, Cripple Creek, Black Hawk, and Central City. They describe how twentieth-century political forces combined to outlaw gambling and its associated vices, although several of the mining towns continued to tolerate the activity.

According to state regulators, legal horse racing in the Rocky Mountain state dates back to 1948. In 1963, the Colorado legislature created a separate State Racing Commission, giving it the authority to license and regulate horse- and dog-racing events and related pari-mutuel wagering. During the 1960s and 1970s, Colorado, like many other pari-mutuel states, benefited from expanded public interest, and participation, in pari-mutuel gambling. By the 1980s, however, Colorado Racing Commission records show that the state's tracks had begun to experience the kind of declines seen in New Jersey, Illinois, and many other states.

In 1983, Colorado became only the third western state (behind Arizona and Washington) to begin a state lottery. The first tickets were sold in January of that year; by April, the state's first million-dollar jackpot was awarded. Colorado's lottery proved successful throughout the decade, and the state followed the typical pattern of expanding the games in both size and scope. "Lotto" was authorized by the General Assembly in 1988, and in April of 1989, the first big "Lotto" prizewinners were announced: a man and a woman from

Denver split the $7 million prize. By April 1999, the State Lottery Commission touted the fact that it had returned $1 billion in proceeds to the state (Colorado Lottery Commission, 2001).

On several occasions, Colorado has altered the statutory requirements pertaining to distribution of state lottery funds. In a 1992 amendment to the state constitution, voters approved the current formula, which allocates 10 percent to state parks, 40 percent to the state's Conservation Trust Fund, and up to 50 percent (but no more than $35 million in constant 1992 dollars) to the Great Outdoors Colorado (GOCO) Trust Fund. GOCO is required, through a competitive grant process, to distribute these funds evenly to state parks, wildlife, open spaces, and local parks and recreation. Debate over the creation of the GOCO trust fund and the use of lottery proceeds is ongoing.

Colorado, like many other states, experienced a flattening of lottery revenue growth in the late 1980s and early 1990s (Sanko, 1989). At the same time, several states, including regional neighbor South Dakota, were considering various new forms of gambling to generate new revenues and economic development. State legislators whose districts included the old mining towns were particularly interested in South Dakota's actions.

The road to legalization for limited-stakes casino gambling included several twists and turns. A 1980 attempt to place a pro-casino amendment on the ballot failed following charges that its supporters had ties to unsavory characters and Las Vegas interests. Similar moves failed in 1982 and 1984 (Dombrink & Thompson, 1990, p. 153). These early failures created latent support for casino gambling in Colorado (Stokowski, 1996, p. 12). Then in 1989, several town leaders in Central City came together one week after casinos in Deadwood, South Dakota, were opened and began studying the possibility of replicating the move (Garner, 1989). Before long, other historic mining towns began to join the effort to bring gambling back. Most already had limited tourism; in the warm summer months vacationers visited Gold Rush–themed attractions where they panned for gold and heard tales of Old West characters as they dined or stayed at local motels.

Gambling in Colorado today bears little resemblance to the original version that began on October 1, 1991. The measure was billed as a way to revitalize the three dying towns by refurbishing their crumbling Victorian buildings into gambling parlors with a period theme.

The extent of financial difficulty the four towns faced prior to gambling was extreme.

According to a newspaper column by a Colorado State Senator: "It is hoped that tourists will come to these towns, not only to engage in limited gambling, but to stay in the hotels, eat in the restaurants, and shop in the stores" (Hopper, S., 1990, April 13). *Weekly Register—Call*, p. 2.). A content analysis of newspaper letters to the editor in the gaming towns just before and during the adoption debates found that residents expressed a "rhetoric of despair" that rose steadily as the adoption campaign progressed (Stokowski, 1996, p. 74).

As the plans began to take shape, so did the initial opposition. It was not long before Governor Roy Romer joined church leaders, law enforcement officials, and others to announce his opposition to the plan.

As the date of the referendum neared, state residents saw stories about the potential gains and losses to be had from gaming. "The towns emphasize that their plans don't include casinos—just slot machines, blackjack and poker tucked into corners of existing businesses, with bets limited to $5," an article in the *Denver Rocky Mountain News* reported (Massaro, 1990, p. 2). Even so, a companion article stated that gambling had already brought so much money into Deadwood, South Dakota, that it was pushing out all other businesses and changing the face of the town ("Officials Visit Deadwood," 1990, p. 2).

Proponents began to challenge the motives and integrity of opponents in an attempt to divert public attention away from the "hard" public policy issues that gambling entailed. "By diverting attention from sensitive issues associated with gambling development . . . and by relying on the rhetoric of despair, proponents successfully created a problem in need of a resolution. . . . Their skill in manipulating the campaign allowed almost everyone to buy into some part of the proposal" (Stokowski, 1996, p. 86).

Voters in 1990 passed by 57 percent to 43 percent the state constitutional amendment that allows limited-stakes gaming in the specified mountain towns.

The original regulatory structure was quite restrictive. Casinos could operate between 8:00 A.M. and 2:00 A.M. seven days per week. The stakes were limited to $5 per bet with no loss limit. Slots, blackjack, and poker were the only games available. Furthermore, "only 35 percent of the total square footage of each casino, and no more

than 50 percent of any given floor, [was to be] devoted to gaming"
(Larsen, 1995, p. 6). Taxes were calculated on a graduated scale,
ranging from a low of 2 percent to a high of 18 percent. Local government assessments varied, and included such items as parking,
sewer, water, and device fees (Larsen, 1995, p. 7).

The growth of casino revenue in Colorado has been phenomenal,
although it has not been steady. In October 1991, the state had 11
gambling halls in three towns, which generated revenue of $8.4 mil-
lion in their first month (Colorado Gaming Commission, 2001). By
September 1992, the number peaked at 76 establishments. In 1997,
some state legislators expressed concern for the future of the industry,
as Harrah's announced its decision to pull out of the Colorado market
("Harrah's: Goodbye Colorado," 1997). In June 2000, there were
only 46 casinos remaining, but there were many large full-service
facilities, such as the Isle of Capri in Black Hawk, with 1,100 slot
machines, 1,000 covered parking spaces, and a 237-room hotel. Col-
lectively, the state's casinos generated record monthly revenues of
$52.8 million (Lane, 2000).

In order to keep some casino firms from leaving the state, the Gaming Commission took steps on several occasions to cut taxes and fees.
In 1994, for example, regulators lowered rates on some smaller casinos from 14 percent to 11.57 percent (Keating, 1994, p. C-01).
Non-live play keno machines were authorized in 1997, and in June
1999, the Gaming Commission completely overhauled its tax and fee
structure, eliminating the $75 per slot machine device fee and insti-
tuting a sliding scale tax structure ranging from 0.25 percent to 20
percent for establishments grossing over $15 million (Colorado Gam-
ing Commission, 2001).

The new structure is reaping big rewards for state coffers but may
not be enough to save gaming in the less-popular locations. Of the
39 casinos that have opened in Central City, only 7 remain. The
historic buildings that were restored and occupied are again empty
and falling into disrepair. Cripple Creek, 40 miles west of Colorado
Springs, has 19 casinos operating, but 31 others have closed. The
town's gaming business has consolidated into a niche market catering
mostly to Colorado Springs and Pueblo, too far from Denver to draw
much of its business or much interest from developers of larger casinos.

Many in deteriorating Central City believe Colorado officials aban-
doned the gaming amendment's original spirit of historic preservation

when big money arrived: "We have all these buildings that are the core of Colorado history, and they're empty. And they keep building new ones. . . . Now it's so far out of hand, all they see is the almighty dollar that it's generating for the state," according to one local resident (quoted in Foster, 2000, p. 3).

Clearly, the trend in Colorado is toward larger, resort-style casino developments with locations that can attract urban day-trip visitors and tourists. The fate of the smaller towns and their historic casinos is uncertain.

Two tribal casinos operate in Colorado as well. In September 1992, the Ute Mountain Casino opened near Towaoc. One year later, the Southern Ute tribe opened its own casino, the Sky Ute Casino and Lodge, near Ignacio, about 25 miles southeast of Durango. The state's compacts with the tribes stipulate that the same $5 bet limits will be applied on tribal lands, although they can operate 24 hours a day and may offer live keno. The compacts also provide mechanisms for the tribes to litigate disputes, including disputes over the limited stakes agreement ("Tribal Gaming," 2001).

The combined effects of a solid state lottery, thriving casino resorts and Indian gaming, and the struggling (yet still surviving) historic casinos and pari-mutuel facilities are clear on the Colorado political scene. The state's need for revenues has outstripped other policy goals with respect to legal gambling. Lawmakers and even voters may have originally wanted historic preservation and capital expansion. Those motives appear to have been set aside in favor of overall revenue growth. Even in the case of the Colorado lottery, which funds such worthy policies as conservation and parks, it is noteworthy that funds in excess of the $35 million cap for the GOCO trust are to flow into the state's general fund.

Louisiana: *"Laissez les bons temps rouler!"*

Gambling in Louisiana is on a roll; and in Cajun country, most residents think that is the way it ought to be. Louisiana has a long and colorful history of promoting sin—from gambling, to drinking, to Mardis Gras—and it has an equally long history of political corruption. Governor Edwin Edwards was no exception. A four-term governor and the populist son of a Cajun sharecropper, Edwards was the target of a dozen federal and state investigations through the years but managed to steer his way around a 1985 indictment on federal racketeering charges (Thomas, 1985, p. 29). However, unable to stay clear of trouble, in January 2001, Edwards, along with his son, was convicted and sentenced to ten years on similar charges relating to riverboat casino locations in the state.

Edwards also can claim at least partial responsibility for letting the (gambling) good times roll. Although casinos were illegal in Louisiana until 1991, the former governor is no stranger to the gaming tables. After winning the governor's office in 1983, Edwards chartered two jumbo jets, talked supporters into paying him large contributions (to help with campaign debts), and then flew the entire group to Monte Carlo (Thomas, 1985, p. 29). He even admitted on a CBS *60 Minutes* broadcast that he had amassed $400,000 in gambling debts in Las Vegas.

The massive Louisiana lottery mail fraud scandal of the 1840s resulted in a statewide constitutional prohibition on gambling (Ezell, 1960, p. 240). Yet, economic pressures in the 1870s caused the state to allow one of the nation's first horse-racing tracks: the Fair Grounds in New Orleans. The track, for a time, attracted a steady stream of both residents and tourists, but since the early 1990s has seen significant declines in revenues.

The declines can probably be attributed to a combination of factors, including a general decline in the pari-mutuel industry, but significant interstate and intrastate competition has surely played a part. In October 1990, voters in Louisiana removed the constitutional ban on the lottery, due at least in part to the success of the Florida lottery and the similar vote that occurred in nearby Texas. At least four other bills to begin a lottery had failed in the previous decade, but the loss of revenues from oil and gas severance taxes in 1988 and 1989 gave lottery supporters a "hook" that residents finally decided to take. Lottery supporters touted gambling as a way to increase revenue collections from tourists and other "outsiders" in newspaper editorials and articles (e.g., see "Casino to Be Built," 1993, p. 1).

Perhaps in response to these tax-shifting arguments, as early as May 1989, statewide polls show that 70 percent of residents favored the creation of a statewide lottery (Katz, 1989, p. A5). In its first 18 months of operation, the Louisiana lottery provided $216.5 million badly needed money for the state treasury, and sales along the state's borders and in tourist-filled New Orleans were especially brisk. In its second year of operation (1992), the Louisiana lottery netted close to $250 million.

The state's lottery revenues have both risen and fallen, but in general are doing well. The addition of "Powerball" in 1994 boosted sales dramatically. Lottery revenues have never again been as high as they were in 1992, but instead have tended to hover around the $150 million mark.

The state's 1991 riverboat gambling law authorizes 15 boats statewide, with no more than 6 to be located in any one parish. As of May 1993, six projects received approval, including one New Orleans project. Three New Orleans land casino projects initially failed miserably, with Harrah's casino closing in November 1995, just seven months after it opened. Although Harrah's has reopened, a number of news stories and financial reports suggest that the New Orleans land-based casino continues to struggle financially. These failures provide our first evidence that market timing is important; it appears the New Orleans casinos were unable to draw many gamblers away from established dockside casinos in nearby Gulfport and Biloxi, Mississippi.

Riverboat gambling in Louisiana has fared better than the land-based casinos. The riverboats provide an excellent example of the multiple ways in which gambling can be viewed as a boon for the state. The legislation was written with an eye toward riverboat gaming as an economic development strategy. It called for all the riverboats to be newly built and prohibited the retrofitting of existing boats. Final legislation amended an earlier version that would have required all the riverboat casinos to be built in Louisiana; even with this amendment, the majority of the boats were built by shipyards in the state.

Such economic windfalls have been widely publicized by the state legislature and chamber of commerce and thus appear to help shore up public support for a revenue producer that residents view as falling most heavily on tourists.

A September 21, 1996, ballot measure put forth by Republican Governor Mike Foster gave Louisiana voters a chance to announce publicly how they feel about gambling in their state. The measure banned any expansion of gambling without specific voter consent. It was followed on November 5, 1996, with local-option votes on whether to keep or drop legal gambling in each parish. While 52 percent of residents casting ballots opposed the gambling in their parishes, and a few parishes banned existing video poker, most of these votes resulted in support for continuation of existing gambling in the state.

The various forms of gambling combined bring the state of Lou-

isiana over $2 billion annually. With 15 riverboat casino licenses au-
thorized, plus a large land-based casino in New Orleans, casinos
provide substantial opportunities for visitors and residents alike. Several thousand video poker machines are available at locations as varied
as truck stops, restaurants, and racetracks. The state's lottery continues to cater to a solid following as well. The factors of economic
competition, public opinion shifts, and a desire to clean up gambling's image are all clearly visible even as the good times roll on in
Louisiana.

Alabama: Citizen Legislators and Special Interest Groups Collide

The headlines heralded the victory: "Lt. Gov. Don Siegelman rode
his proposal for a state lottery to victory over Republican Gov. Fob
James. One of the few Democrats to oust an incumbent Republican
governor this year, Siegelman won 58 percent to James's 42 percent,
with 99 percent of precincts reporting," was the way the Associated
Press reported it (AP News Online, 1998). This story, and most others like it, went on to explain how polls clearly showed that support
of the Alabama Lottery for Education proposal was a primary factor
in voters' decisions to send Siegelman to the Montgomery governor's
mansion.

The punch line to the story probably surprised no one more than
it did Siegelman; in the required statewide ballot on the issue, voters
subsequently rejected the lottery for education. Why? The answers
that have been given in the major news media have tended to focus
on two specific issues. First, there is the strong anti-lottery push fi-
nanced by a number of pro-family and conservative Christian groups.
Second, questions have been raised by those groups and other political opponents of the lottery about the ethics of the proposed plan.

Prior to 1999, Alabama has had only limited public discussion of
gambling policy. Currently the state allows the operation of bingo,
heavily regulated and allowable in most counties only when operated
for charities (Yardley, 1993), as well as pari-mutuels in the form of
three greyhound racetracks and one combined horse and dog track
(Christiansen, 1999, p. 4).

When the Mobile Greyhound Park opened in 1973, it was the only
legal pari-mutuel gambling facility in the state (Bolton, 1993). As of
1993, the state has three additional dog-racing facilities in Greene,

Macon, and Jefferson counties. Victoryland, opened in 1984 in Macon County, was the nation's most successful dog track in 1987, but has since been hurt by the addition of dog racing at the existing horse-racing track in Birmingham; the opening of casino gambling in Biloxi, Mississippi in late 1992 (Bolton, 1993, p. 10); and the start of nearby Georgia's state lottery in July 1993.

The Birmingham Race Track, approved in 1984, was the second horse-racing facility in the Deep South, following Louisiana. Although faced with some resistance when first proposed, the track drew enough public support to win both a statewide constitutional amendment vote in November 1984 (Grimm, 1984) and a Birmingham city referendum in June of the same year (Schmidt, 1984).

Several times in the early 1990s, members of the Alabama legislature have proposed expanding the allowable forms of gambling to include such things as a state lottery, casino-style dockside gaming, and casino- or lottery-style video terminals to be placed at existing pari-mutuel facilities, a move meant to bolster state revenues and track attendance (Bolton, 1993, p.10). None of these efforts was successful, due at least in part to a legislature that was distracted by a series of political scandals and the settlement of an education reform lawsuit. Through the 1990s, it appeared that the reasons for Alabama's failure to catch on to the rapid "third wave" (Rose, 1991) of gambling lay not so much with voters as with legislators, who in their brief annual sessions have in the past decade faced far more pressing decisions. The lottery idea also did not have the backing, during the early part of the decade, of state legislative leaders.

Owners of the pari-mutuel facilities, as well as the county and city executives, who depend on them for tax revenues, have not opposed proposals that would incorporate the existing tracks. The politically powerful owner of two of the state's racetracks, Milton McGregor, put it this way: "To protect the thousands of jobs in this industry in our state, we have to offer what our competition offers and the Mississippi casinos and the Indian reservations are our competition. . . . When we have people from Georgia, who have been coming to Victoryland since it opened, start bypassing us and driving another three hours to Mississippi and passing two dog tracks on the way, we have a problem" (quoted in Bolton, 1993, p. 10).

Through the early 1990s, lottery bills were introduced each year by a Montgomery County state legislator, Representative Alvin Holmes; yet, they never came up for a vote. Why have voters in other states been able to get the legal gambling they wanted, often over the opposition of elected officials? One answer may lie in direct democracy processes such as initiative, referendum, and recall. None of these is available to Alabama voters, so while a majority of voters may have wanted a lottery or other forms of gambling, they lacked any straightforward mechanism by which to force the issue to a vote. Lobbying is the only real method of attempting to influence policy in Alabama. However, additional forms of gambling in Alabama also have failed to attract support from any major interest groups.

Rather than offer their support, several important groups have in the past actively opposed lotteries. Bill Smith, president of the A+ Organization, which has pushed for education reform in the state, opposed several lottery bills, as has the Alabama Education Association (AEA), the state's powerful education lobby. The AEA only joined the push for a lottery after Siegelman made it a cornerstone in his campaign to oust Governor Fob James. By contrast, education officials in Florida, Georgia, and Texas have all been behind their state's lottery movements early on ("Gambling in the South, II," 1993, p. 2-A). Milton McGregor's political organization, called JOB-PAC, had been reported to be lobbying against a lottery because he feared it might further siphon away gambling dollars from his pari-mutuel tracks (Patriquin, 1994, p. A1).

Another key to the lack of work on legal gambling during this period may have been the lack of a strong gubernatorial push. As the examples in states such as Illinois and Louisiana clearly demonstrate, proposed gambling legalization often comes from governors (and gubernatorial candidates). Until 1999, no governor or strong gubernatorial candidate had ever proposed a state lottery. Democratic Governor Jim Folsom came close when he declared in August 1993 that he wanted the legislature to take up the issue of a state lottery in a special session that he called for August 23 that year. State legislators, already in special session to reform state ethics and campaign finance laws, encouraged him to reconsider, since they would not have had enough time to deal with all three issues. A similar measure failed to gain legislative approval in 1996 ("Gambling Under Attack," 1996, p. 783).

Again, the state's powerful racetrack owner Milton McGregor also may have played a part. His contributions to various Alabama governors have raised eyebrows among some voters in the state, and created concern for any attempt by the governor to promote the adoption of additional forms of gambling (Patriquin, 1994, p. A1). His only major gambling competition in the state—Greenetrack in Eutaw—had to close live racing operations in the late summer of 1996 because of poor attendance.

An attempt to create a lottery for education modeled after the highly successful Georgia lottery began in 1992. But the failure to move forward quickly with such a plan may have sown the seeds of undoing for Governor Siegelman's plan two and a half years later. During the second half of the 1990s, a number of local newspaper articles, television news segments, and national media attention focused on the state lotteries, particularly those in places such as Florida and Georgia. While some supporters thought that this attention might make it easier to pass legislation in states such as Alabama, the evidence supports the opposite conclusion as well. Several articles in state newspapers detailed how education funding in Florida had not grown since the lottery was begun, and others explained how some educators in Georgia are resentful of the state's use of lottery funds only in college scholarships, pre-K programs, and technology upgrades.

These concerns provided specific fodder for anti-lottery forces, and many times opponents quoted directly from these stories. The 1999 release of the National Gambling Impact Study Commission report and the subsequent intense discussions of potential social ills associated with gambling provided more fuel for the anti-lottery fires.

When the time came for the new governor to actually propose a plan, anti-lottery forces were ready. They formed coalitions and began to devise a grassroots strategy to defeat the lottery, although many acknowledge that they never dreamed they would be so successful. One such group—Citizens Against Legalized Lottery (CALL)—reported that they and other opponents spent over $1 million on advertising, billboards, and flyers. Pro-lottery forces, however, backed by the state Democratic Party and educational associations, outspent CALL three-to-one ("Lottery Vote Shows," 1999).

On the surface, the Siegelman lottery plan was quite similar to Georgia's. It provided that lottery proceeds be used only to pay for college scholarships for students with a grade point average of B or better; funding a new public, pre-kindergarten program; and improving technology in Alabama's public schools. Like Georgia's plan, the Alabama plan did not specifically describe which forms of lottery games (scratch-off, instant-draw keno games, lottos) would be allowed. Those decisions were left open for the new Alabama Education Lottery Corporation to determine. Unlike the Georgia law, the Alabama proposal would not have specified winning rates (in Georgia, half of all lottery proceeds must be returned as prizes). In the Alabama plan, only administrative expense levels were set (no higher than 20 percent or 20 cents on the dollar).

What was troubling for many in the state was that the Alabama lottery plan had what some viewed as a rather lax set of standards for contracting of lottery services—the most lucrative part of a statewide lottery, and the part most subject to ethical scrutiny. In a *Mobile Register* story following the ballot defeat of the proposal, political scientist Sam Fisher of the University of South Alabama said that the lottery proposal tended to "reinforce the image that this money is going to provide money to the old crew, the good old boys" ("Could It?" 1999).

Opponents used this notion in their anti-lottery television advertising—suggesting that Governor Siegelman had purposely structured the bill in such a way as to help some of his cronies. The same story also noted that "opponents also claimed that a recent traffic ticket-fixing scandal showed that the Democratic governor's administration could not be trusted to oversee gambling in the state" ("Could It?" 1999).

Was the governor and his trustworthiness, or lack of it, the key issue? Most supporters and opponents have publicly acknowledged that the morality of state lotteries was the central issue dividing supporters and opponents. Alabama Education Association Executive Chairman Ron Hubbard, in an interview following the lottery defeat, said that it was very hard to stand up against the churches and their leaders, and that it was they who put up the strongest fight. "It was a battle of morals. . . . They got their people out to the polls" ("Could It?" 1999).

Certainly, the pro-lottery forces had reason to raise the question of church involvement. Several of the state's polling operations have asked Alabama residents' opinions regarding various gambling proposals. When asked, questions about proposed lotteries have typically received the agreement or support of a majority of the respondents. Other proposed forms of gambling, such as riverboat casinos and video gambling, also have received substantial support from voters.

State polls in 1983, 1985, 1987, 1988, 1989, 1990, 1992, 1993, 1994, and 1998 have asked various questions about legalized gam-

bling. Of these, one of the most extensive is the 1993 poll by Southern Opinion Research (SOR). In order to ascertain respondents'
support for a number of hypothetical forms of gambling, the poll
asks: "Several proposals have recently been made about establishing
different types of legal gambling in Alabama. Do you approve or
disapprove of the following types of legalized gambling being permitted in Alabama?" Then a list of seven possible forms of gambling
is read, and the respondent answers with either "agree," "disagree,"
or "don't know." The results of these polls are summarized in Table
3.3. In the 1989 survey, 63 percent of Alabama residents said they
favored a state lottery, and that figure increased to 74 percent when
the question specifically mentioned earmarking lottery monies for education. A majority, 52 percent, in the 1992 survey favored riverboat
casino gambling, but support fell to only 41 percent for "casino gambling," which is a less-defined option.

SOR and the University of Alabama's Capstone Poll (CAP) specifically tracked support for a state lottery in Alabama between 1983
and 1998. In 13 separate polls, they asked: "In order to raise more
money, should the state government in Alabama have a lottery?" or
some very similarly worded variant.[3] The total percentage of persons
in Alabama expressing support for the state lottery grew steadily between 1983 and 1992, and then declined steadily but less sharply,
until 1998. From nothing more than a simple examination of these
data, it would appear that lottery supporters missed their opportunity
to bring the statewide game to Alabama when they failed to act in
the early 1990s.

Table 3.3 also shows the percent of persons supporting other gambling forms during the period. Unfortunately, the polls did not typically include questions about whether respondents were of the
Christian faith, nor did they ask about church attendance. However,
demographic data from the polls suggests that support from the lottery came from all sectors.

One Protestant pastor from Bay Minette was quoted in the Mobile
papers as saying he believed his congregation would have easily supported the lottery if it had been targeted toward K–12 education,
rather than college scholarships ("Could It?" 1999). Of particular
interest is a poll conducted in June 1992. Along with the question
about support for a state lottery, this poll described various ideas
associated with legal gambling and asked respondents whether they
agreed or disagreed with them. The results in Table 3.3 suggest that

Table 3.3
Alabama Residents' Support for a Statewide Lottery and Other Gambling, 1988–1992

Lottery Questions

Date	Poll	Percent Approving
5/1983	CAP	45
10/1985	CAP	59
5/1987	CAP	58
7/1989	SOR	58
7/1989	SOR	63
5/1990	SOR	66
6/1992	SOR	66
8/1994	SOR	63
9/1994	SOR	62
8/1998	SOR	62
9/1998	SOR	57 [67 for scholarship]
10/1998	SOR	55 [61 scholarship]
10/1998	SOR	52 [64 scholarship]

Other Gambling Form Questions

7/1989	SOR	
Ever been to a casino?		35 (Yes)
Ever bought a lottery ticket?		36 (Yes)

Support for:	(6/1992 SOR)
Bingo for cash	67
Casino gambling	41
Video gambling	47
OTB races	39
Bet on sports . . .	42
Riverboat casinos	52

Percent agreeing with these statements:	(6/1992 SOR)
Gambling provides needed $ for educ.	60
It makes compulsive gamblers . . .	52
It creates jobs	68
It encourages people to gamble . . .	58
It is immoral	42

moral issues were of concern to Alabama residents well before the churches began actively opposing Siegelman's plan.

For example, while 60 percent of poll respondents agreed that gambling is one way to provide needed funds for education, 58 percent thought state action legalizing gambling would encourage persons to gamble who might not otherwise do so. While the question about the morality of gambling was essentially a statistical tie, 52 percent thought it makes compulsive gamblers out of some people who would not otherwise become so.

The most relevant of the SOR polls for our purposes were conducted in September and October 1998. A question about the establishment of a state lottery for Alabama received about 55 percent on each of these polls. Nevertheless, when the question was asked specifically about a lottery to provide college scholarships, support rose to about 65 percent. These questions were asked just prior to the gubernatorial election, and many interpreted such results at the time as suggesting that the lottery issue provided voters for Siegelman. It now seems relevant to ask the question whether support for Siegelman (and/or opposition to the incumbent governor Fob James) may have provided support for the lottery-for-education idea.

In other words, Alabama voters may have wanted, in October 1998, someone new to come in and make some changes, particularly in the area of education. After nearly four years of Governor James—years during which many educators felt their concerns had been ignored—Siegelman had arrived on the scene offering concrete suggestions. For those voters (and we could assume for the sake of argument that there were many) who had not personally studied state lotteries and who knew relatively little about them other than the anecdotal stories from nearby Georgia and Florida, a state lottery for education probably sounded like an appealing idea.

The talk during the time in fact was framed in "easy" terms. As a candidate, Siegelman repeatedly told voters to "look at Georgia's success," with the lottery. SOR pollsters Patrick Cotter and James Stovall said in a 1998 election analysis: "Siegelman's emphasis on the lottery forced James to respond. His belated scholarship plan was weak and not credible. His opposition to the idea of a lottery, while it may have heartened some of his hardcore Christian conservative supporters, put him on the wrong side of this issue with two-thirds of the electorate" (Cotter & Stovall, 1998).

In the year that followed, much more evidence and detail were provided to Alabama residents about state lotteries, in general, and about the model of Georgia's lottery, in particular. The issue became complicated. Thus, with this newly acquired information, a small but significant portion of Alabama voters now had changed their minds about the lottery as an answer to the state's educational problems. It became easier to oppose the lottery than it was to figure out who was right about it. That shift of 5 or 10 percent of voters could easily translate into a much larger shift at the polls if turnout was high among (motivated) opponents, and low among supporters.

The evidence provides support for such a scenario. While there is certainly truth in the charge that fundamentalist and evangelical Protestant churches lobbied vigorously—with ministers providing direction from the pulpit for their congregants to vote against the lottery—there is also sufficient evidence that such persons were never strongly in favor of the lottery in significant numbers to begin with. While ethical concerns might have chipped away at the governor's own base, again, they probably were not needed to convince the fundamentalists. It is unlikely that many strong evangelicals and fundamentalists would have voted for the lottery anyway.

What shifted, as is so often the case with ballot measures, were the "moderates" and "soft supporters" on the lottery issue. Ethical considerations about who plays the lottery, how much lottery funds would help improve education in the state, whether the proposal itself was a solid and well-written piece of legislation, all were of concern to moderates who were among those who generally did not feel lotteries are immoral. Thus "morals," as typically defined, probably did not hold sway so much as did relevant policy concerns.

Many of the same precincts that heavily supported Seigelman, over then-incumbent Governor Fob James, in 1998 soundly defeated the lottery proposal, according to Paul Johnson of Auburn University (Johnson, 2000). The *Birmingham News* reported that one precinct in northwest Alabama where Seigelman won by 4,000 votes in 1998 rejected Seigelman's lottery plan by almost 4,500 votes.

Will the Alabama experience impact the gambling policy debates in future situations? The likely answer is a resounding yes. For pro-gambling forces to hold sway, they must first gain support of their own political base (those who stand most to benefit either politically or economically from the proposed gambling form as well as those who personally want the opportunity to gamble legally). They must also convince those persons who tend to "sit on the fence" on the gambling issue. Antigambling forces now understand that "hard" issues are easier to defeat, so they will likely provide mountains of technical detail about gambling proposals and their possible impacts. If pro-gambling forces cannot come up with compelling arguments against these positions, we may begin to see more setbacks in the expansion of legal gambling.

Conclusions

Examining the decision-making process in five states regarding legalization of various forms of gambling suggests several factors may be at work. First, as the theory developed in Chapters 1 and 2 suggests, there is the public. Voters in four of these states were asked to amend their constitutions to allow gambling. Legislators appear to prefer the political cover that such votes can provide.

Where majorities of voters have expressed a desire for a certain type of gambling, and where opinion leaders have been able to reframe gambling in easy terms, the state's policy process has worked to give voters what they want. Gambling as gambling has a much more difficult time attracting and keeping majority public support, particularly in those parts of the country that tend to be more socially conservative, such as the South, than does gambling as education funding, for example. The effect and level of support or opposition by key groups within the public is crucial here. Support for the idea of a lottery or casino in the abstract may be a very different thing from support for a specific proposal. Thus, some proxy of the likely amount of resistance, such as membership in fundamentalist religious groups, is probably a far more reliable predictor of gambling policy adoption than direct measures of public opinion.

However, as the Alabama case illustrates, expressed majority public support for proposed gambling is not enough to ensure policy adoption, even when some leaders attempt to frame the issue in easy terms; other factors can combine to make specific gambling proposals less attractive, and thus cause their demise. Opponents can use areas of weakness, such as Alabama Governor Siegelman's alleged improprieties in planning to award contracts to political cronies, to mobilize "consensus" opinion to defeat gambling. Gambling's history of corruption requires, just as it did in both New Jersey and Colorado, that casino or lottery adoptions appear to be free of influence from criminal or corrupt elements.

The process also appears to be shaped by revenue and overall economic development policy concerns: The casino adoptions in New Jersey, Colorado, Illinois, and Louisiana came at a time when serious economic needs outstripped the ability of existing state taxes to meet those needs. Both Illinois and Colorado passed state lotteries in years marked by economic downturn, and Louisiana's lottery was authorized on the cusp of a recession. Clearly, when states are facing a revenue crisis, state leaders are likely to actively promote gambling, and gambling should be much more likely to pass.

The perceived level of competition from other states was apparently a factor in the debates of New Jersey, Illinois, Colorado, and Louisiana. Other policy issues matter; in the case of casinos, there are very real concerns over location and spin-off social policy impacts. The Alabama case reveals that serious consideration was given by many voters to the lottery's potential to divert a portion of many residents' limited incomes from necessities to the lottery. A number of newspaper editorials urged residents to vote against the lottery because of its regressive nature. Thus, the level of resources available to the state might be one consideration of state legislators and voters in gambling adoption decisions.

Even in Alabama, the case studies revealed that gambling, once legalized, brings its own constituencies, which serve to further support its entrenchment in society. Alabama pari-mutuel track owners, along with the communities in which those tracks are located, have continued to lobby state lawmakers for gambling expansions, such as legalization of video poker or slot machines, which they view as potentially beneficial to their business. All the while, these same groups have quietly worked to oppose a statewide lottery, which they tend to view as potentially harmful to their bottom line. In Colorado and Illinois, gambling that was initially limited was allowed and even encouraged by state regulators to spread. Thus, measures of competition and the presence of other legal gambling forms would be likely to impact adoption outcomes.

These case studies confirm that several forms of gambling under consideration have been presented to the public in economic development terms, and that explicit attempts have been made by supporters to downplay or shift public discussion away from the underlying moral questions associated with gambling, as in the case of Colorado. This evidence provides support for the notion that gambling policy is moving toward "consensus morality policy" (Meier,

1999). The discussion of Louisiana's riverboat casino authorization highlights this point well. That law explicitly attempts to use the occasion of riverboat adoption as a window of economic development opportunity. Illinois' placement of casino riverboats along state borders is another example.

Finally, it is clear from the cases that the various forms of gambling differ in terms of the political situations that surround debates over adoption or expansion. States such as Colorado, Illinois, and Louisiana that have adopted multiple forms of gambling have experienced very different adoption campaigns, centered on different issues and concerns, as each new gambling form has been made legal. While some key groups opposing gambling may remain the same, they have tended to change their tactics and rhetoric to suit the form of gambling under consideration. These case studies have also provided some insight into the factors that lead states to adopt gambling, particularly the quest for new and relatively painless revenues, and they hint at the decision process faced by states as they consider the various forms of gambling.

AUTHORIZING LEGISLATION AND THE POLITICS OF ADOPTION

A number of articles in various journals over the past decade have examined the political forces behind expanded legalization of statewide lotteries (Berry and Berry, 1990; Caudill, Ford, Mixon, & Peng, 1995; McKinney & Swain, 1993; Pierce & Miller, 2001; Winn & Whicker, 1989; Wohlenberg, 1992). Since 1989, however, an area of much faster growth has been the legalization of casinos in the states. At the end of 1999, casinos were touting their success as employers of over 325,000 employees and payers of over $2.5 billion in direct gaming tax revenues (American Gaming Association, 1999).

A classic book examines the political history of the adoptions of, and failures to adopt, casinos in a number of states (Dombrink & Thompson, 1990). Individual states' casinos are examined in other books: New Jersey (Demaris, 1986; Pollock, 1987; Sternlieb & Hughes, 1983), Colorado, (Stokowski, 1996), and, of course, Nevada (Farrell & Case, 1995; Glass, 1981; Moehring, 1989). In other recent publications, the revenue impacts of California card rooms have been examined (Sutphen, Grant, & Ball, 1994), and the tax incidence of casinos in Mississippi has been estimated (Rivenbark &

Rounsaville, 1996). Casinos in Mississippi have also been shown to be the catalyst for increased sales tax collections in gaming locales (Clynch & Rivenbark, 1999).

The Annals of the American Academy of Political and Social Science has devoted entire issues to gambling, the most recent of which included articles on casinos' impacts on local economies (Eadington, 1998), on state economies (Gazel, 1998), on community development (Blevins & Jensen, 1998), and on street crime (Miller & Schwartz, 1998).

While these books and articles present important findings about the impacts of casinos, the political science community has tended to ignore the politics of casinos. By twisting and paraphrasing Harold Lasswell's oft-quoted definition, the present study asks the question: "Who gets casinos, when, and how?" This section particularly addresses questions one through three of the morality policy process model about the participants, their expectations, and their interactions.

There appears to be no specific regional pattern to the adoption of casinos. The tables in Chapter 2 show the adoptions of both casinos and lotteries. Some form of casino is now available within 500 miles of most U.S. residents.[4] An interesting question is: What factor(s) can account for the unprecedented growth of casinos between 1988 and the present? In addition, it is worth considering what factors led some states to adopt casinos while others chose to add lotteries during the same period.

The Lottery and Casino Adoption Literature

Although not extensive, there exists a fairly robust and cohesive literature on the factors that lead states to adopt lotteries, as I have discussed. These articles and books, which appeared mainly in the late 1980s and very early 1990s, examine the adoption decisions of states choosing lotteries prior to 1989. At least two of these researchers found that the earliest states to adopt were primarily in the Northeast, whereas Western and Midwestern states were more likely to adopt lotteries during the 1980s (Clotfelter & Cook, 1989; Wohlenberg, 1992). States adopting since publication of these earlier studies have primarily been in the South and the West.

The lottery adoption literature generally concentrates on a small handful of factors that consistently account for lottery adoptions

throughout the 1970s and 1980s. These include Protestant Fundamentalist Church membership,[5] certain measures of state fiscal health,
and the presence of neighboring states that had previously adopted
lotteries (Berry & Berry, 1990; Winn & Whicker, 1989; Wohlenberg,
1992). The methodologies employed range from simple cross-
tabulations (Winn & Whicker, 1989) to complex event history analysis (EHA) a form of pooled cross-sectional time series analysis
utilizing logit/probit techniques (Berry & Berry, 1990; Caudill,
Ford, Mixon, & Peng, 1995).

At least two articles examining the adoption of casinos have been
published. One uses very simple methodology to examine states'
choice among gambling forms, and finds that generally lotteries and
pari-mutuels conform to one predictive model, whereas casinos appear to conform to another (von Herrmann, 1999). The second looks
at the adoption of casinos, using a simple logistic regression model
and predominantly economic variables (Furlong, 1997).

The Furlong article examines only casinos adopted between 1988
and 1997 (e.g., it excludes both Nevada and New Jersey from its
analysis) and uses indicators derived primarily from pre-1990 data. It
finds, contrary to Berry and Berry (1990), that external competition
does not appear to be a factor in casino adoptions, as it was for lottery
adoptions. The author explains that competition variables performed
so poorly because so few states have yet adopted (Furlong, 1997, p.
376).

Yet, a recent reexamination of the Berry and Berry (1990) piece
questions how well the external determinants (e.g., the regional diffusion factor) can perform once many states have jumped on the lottery bandwagon (Mooney, 2001). While it contains important
theoretical contributions, especially regarding the role that cognitive
screening may play in legislative dealings with the casino issue, the
time-bound nature of Furlong's model (1997) may be at least partly
responsible for his finding, since his simple model cannot accurately
test for pressure from neighboring states' adoptions when these adoptions were generally clustered over a five-year period.

Of all the techniques used by previous researchers, the EHA appears to offer the most helpful findings because it allows a researcher
to simultaneously test both internal factors, such as religious membership and personal incomes, and external (or regional) diffusion
factors, such as competition from neighboring states. The EHA technique also does not suffer from the flaw of time-bound models and,

thus, can more accurately account for the potential building of pressure to adopt caused by increasingly tight budgets or increasing numbers of neighbors that have adopted. Because it is much more versatile and robust, the present research will follow the general design of Berry and Berry's EHA study (1990), replicating and expanding it to explain the adoption of casinos.

Creating a Test of the Politics of Casino Adoption

It remains unclear whether lotteries and casinos are adopted for the same reasons. The earlier lottery adoption literature suggests that fiscal need, low levels of fundamentalist religious membership, regional diffusion, divided party control of state government, the presence of a state election, and possibly state personal income levels are the factors most likely to lead to lottery adoption. The case studies suggest that some of these same concerns are at work with casinos. State fiscal need, religious membership, state income levels (which may be perceived by policy makers as a rough estimate of the level of state social services available), the existence of other forms of legal gambling, and the competitive pressure from neighboring states' lottery or casino adoption are all expected to relate to casino adoptions.

What follows is a replication of Berry and Berry (1990) for the adoption of both lotteries and casinos. The data sources to be examined are the same as in Berry and Berry, and the reader is referred to that article for additional details. In order to simplify the theory, each state is assumed to consider the adoption of a state lottery or a casino, even though practically speaking this may not have been the case.

The risk set, or dependent variable, is confined to the 48 contiguous states in the continental United States because of the desire to check for the influence of neighboring states' decisions. All 48 of these states are initially considered at risk for adopting both a lottery and casino. Furthermore, states remain in the analysis until they have adopted both a lottery and casinos, as seven states, in fact, have. Thus, for a state having adopted neither a casino nor a lottery as of 2000, such as South Carolina or Utah, the time series for the dependent variable has no variation, but is instead a series of zeros starting in 1985 and ending in 1990.[6] The series begins in 1965—the year following New Hampshire's adoption of a lottery—and ends in 1996.

Table 3.4
EHA Test of Gambling Adoptions, 1965–1996

Var.	Lotteries Coeff	Casinos Coeff	Both Coeff
Income	.000412*	.000471**	.000613**
Religion	−2.73283***	−2.62269*	−3.55801*
Fiscal	−.920786*	−.003172	−.026633
Party	−.116059	.011748	−.026904
Lottery1st	.242421**	++++	−.097027
Casino1st	++++	.559447***	.537593***
−Constant	−1.8357***	−2.81361***	−2.745829***
−2 (Log-likel.)^a	49.18***	68.37***	63.99***
Pseudo R^2 ^{b}	.233	.323	.326

*$p < .05$ **$p < .01$ ***$p < .001$

^{a} Minus 2 times the log-likelihood ratio is distributed as chi-square (with 5 degrees of freedom in columns one and two and 6 degrees of freedom in column three).
^{b} Pseudo R^2 as reported by the STATA package probit analysis; see Aldrich and Nelson (1984, p.57–59) for a description of this measure.

Results of the Analysis

The analysis for the adoption of state lotteries, shown in Table 3.4, generally confirms and replicates the earlier findings of Berry and Berry (1990). As might be expected, the variables together explain about 23 percent of the variance in lottery adoptions. The independent variables are all in the hypothesized direction, and the coefficient for the fiscal variable is statistically significant, at least for lotteries.

It appears that lottery adoptions continue to be influenced by state income levels, religious membership of state residents, fiscal health of the adopting state, and the lottery adoption decisions of neighboring states.[7] The results for casinos alone, and for both lotteries and casinos, show that some of the same factors that led states to adopt lotteries can also lead states to adopt casinos. The results are fairly robust: As Table 3.4 shows, the model explains about 32 percent of the variance in state casino adoptions, although this time neither the fiscal nor the party variables have significant coefficients. Finally, a combined model is estimated, as shown in Table 3.4; it accounts for 32 percent of the variance in the adoption of both lotteries and casinos (that is, the likelihood that a state will eventually adopt both). Interestingly, in the full model for explaining which states will adopt both a lottery and a casino, the fiscal and party variables are (again) not statistically significant.

In addition, the model for adopting both a lottery and a casino includes a variable, called Lottery1st, which checks for the likelihood that a state's neighbors had already adopted lotteries. Given the case study finding that casino adopters appeared to be reacting quickly to the adoption decisions of other states, it seemed likely that this would mean these states might have been early adopters of lotteries. Rather than a positive relationship, however, this variable becomes insignificant and takes on the opposite sign from that hypothesized. Examining the data more closely reveals that states that have adopted both lotteries and casinos were generally somewhat "late" to adopt lotteries.

Predicting the Adoption of Casino Gaming

Predicted probabilities of a state adopting a casino[8] (derived from the earlier analysis) for hypothetical states with differing characteristics are presented in Table 3.5.

Based on the results obtained earlier by Berry and Berry (1990), it would seem likely that increased fiscal strain in a state would lead to an increased likelihood of adopting a casino, at least in states with few religious fundamentalists, yet the results do not bear out that hypothesis.

Changing the fiscal health of the state does not change the effects of religious fundamentalism or of personal incomes on the likelihood of a state adopting a casino. The measure of competition from neighbor states, on the other hand, does appear to work in concert with the other variables for religion and income, and there appears to be a small interaction between the income and religion variables as well. The new hypotheses are also tested here about the interaction effects of internal and external factors, and these provide an important new insight into the states' decision process. Neighbors' casino adoption decisions, taken in concert with religious fundamentalism in a state, produce small, but noticeable, changes in the likelihood of adoption. Going from no neighbors adopting to having two neighbors adopt, in a state with low fundamentalist membership, results in an increase of 1.5 percent to the chances of adoption.

Where resources are low, it appears that internal political factors such as religious fundamentalism become slightly more potent. In a state with low levels of religious fundamentalism, the chance of casino adoption would be .001 greater when personal incomes are low than in a similarly situated state with high levels of income. However, for states with large numbers of religious fundamentalists, the change from a state having low personal income levels to a state with higher levels results in a change of .004 in the probability of casino adoption.

In short, religion, income levels, and neighboring states' adoptions all matter in casino adoption decisions. This finding is consistent with earlier research findings from the lottery literature that there are only minuscule effects of fiscal health on gambling adoption decisions when taken in concert with stronger factors such as religious membership and personal income levels.

Conclusions

This test of gambling adoptions has shown that lotteries and casinos are generally adopted by states in similar internal and external situations. States with relatively low numbers of Protestant Fundamentalists and with relatively high personal income levels and those with numerous neighbors who have adopted the same form of gambling are substantially more likely to adopt than states not so situated. It is also noteworthy, though, that the model can account for only a limited amount of the variance in adoption decisions. As much of the morality politics literature proves, state policy adoptions are difficult to explain out of context. That context includes a wide array of historical, political, and personality factors.

These findings also present some interesting and somewhat perplexing questions for those who study or are involved in the gambling industry. If fiscal health of the state is not the prime variable in gambling adoptions (that is, if it is not able to serve as the primary explanatory variable in models such as this one and Berry and Berry's [1990]), why then are the political battles surrounding those adoptions so often framed in terms of revenues? The revenues generated by even the most successful state lotteries and casinos are relatively small when compared to traditional taxes such as sales and income tax (with the noteworthy exception of Nevada casinos, which have historically generated substantial portions of that state's total revenue). Perhaps, as the analysis just presented suggests, fiscal stress may

Table 3.5
Predicted Probabilities of Casino Adoption for Hypothetical States Under Stated Conditions

Hypothetical Condition	Fiscal	Religion	Income	Casino1st	Prob. of adoption
Low Religion; Income and Casino1st held at median levels					
High Fiscal	.015	.071	139.11	1	.003 ◆
Low Fiscal	−.25	.071	139.11	1	.003 ◆
High Religion; Income and Casino1st held at median levels					
High Fiscal	.015	.344	139.11	1	.001
Low Fiscal	−.25	.344	139.11	1	.002
Low Income; Religion and Casino1st held at median levels					
High Fiscal	.015	.176	40.68	1	.002 ◆
Low Fiscal	−.25	.176	40.68	1	.001 ◆
High Income; Religion and Casino1st held at median levels					
High Fiscal	.015	.176	273.37	1	.002 ◆
Low Fiscal	−.25	.176	273.37	1	.002 ◆
Low Casino1st; Religion and Income held at median levels					
High Fiscal	.015	.176	139.11	0	.003 ◆
Low Fiscal	−.25	.176	139.11	0	.003 ◆
High Casino1st; Religion and Income held at median levels					
High Fiscal	.015	.176	139.11	2	.011 ◆
Low Fiscal	−.25	.176	139.11	2	.011 ◆
Low Religion; Fiscal and Income held at median levels					
Low Casino1st	.045	.070	139.11	0	.005
High Casino1st	.045	.070	139.11	2	.019
High Religion; Fiscal and Income held at median levels					
Low Casino1st	.045	.344	139.11	0	.001
High Casino1st	.045	.344	139.11	2	.004
Low Income; Fiscal and Religion held at median levels					
Low Casino1st	.045	.176	40.68	0	.001
High Casino1st	.045	.176	40.68	2	.009
High Income; Fiscal and Religion held at median levels					
Low Casino1st	.045	.176	273.37	0	.001
High Casino1st	.045	.176	273.37	2	.012
Low Income; Fiscal and Casino1st held at median levels					
Low Religion	.045	.070	40.68	1	.002
High Religion	.045	.344	40.68	1	.000

Table 3.5 (*continued*)

Hypothetical Condition	Fiscal	Religion	Income	Casino1st	Prob. of adoption
High Income; Fiscal and Casino1st held at median levels					
Low Religion	.045	*.070*	273.37	1	.003
High Religion	.045	*.34*	273.37	1	.002

* Changing values are italicized; those held constant are in normal type.
◆ Hypothesized effect not found: either no change in the probability or change in
    probability not in the hypothesized direction.

be more a question of timing—particularly in those states where substantial numbers of religious opponents or other mitigating factors are present. In short, in states where gambling is more likely to pass on its own merits, those states are less likely to wait until fiscal need is present. However, in states with substantial opposition, political elites may use the occasion of a fiscal crisis to try to persuade the public to go along with gambling.

Certainly, a question worth considering is whether casinos are being viewed by states primarily as revenue generators, or in some other terms. For casinos, much of the discussion in some states has centered on the economic development possibilities of the casino industry. That was especially true in the early 1990s' adoptions in Colorado and Louisiana. Important questions remain as to the effect of perceived economic development benefits on the outcome of gambling authorizations.

State politics is filled with paradoxes, as anyone who studies it can attest. The case studies of states that have adopted casinos and lotteries presented here reveal that sometimes these policies make odd political bedfellows. In New Jersey, for example, the casinos were adopted only after substantial changes were made to the plan for distributing the revenues—changes which were designed to win the support of the substantial lobby for the elderly in that state.

As the theory sketched in Chapter 1 proposes, this analysis of lottery and casino adoptions shows clearly that gambling is salient, and that while influenced by its history of scandal and morality concerns, gambling is not viewed entirely as an issue of morality politics. Gambling policy falls within the area of morality politics, to be sure, but it, perhaps even more than other issues of morality such as gay rights and drug policy, is viewed equally as an economic policy.

Haider-Markel (1999) describes how lesbian and gay rights issues may fall into either of two prominent categories of morality politics:

one where the influence of interest group resources is difficult to capture empirically and another where influence may be more visible. We might define the first type as "sin" politics—where one advocacy coalition has successfully defined the issue solely in terms of sin. . . . The second type . . . could be defined as "opposing coalition" politics, where two or more advocacy coalitions successfully define an issue in at least two acceptable ways. . . . [I]nterest groups in this case are likely to expend most of their resources attempting to control the scope of the conflict, using issue frames to appeal to broad or narrow constituencies. (747)

Given that duality, gambling politics as observed in these chapters fails to conform well to either model. In some cases, particularly in the earlier adoption stories, the arguments against gambling have been clearly presented in "easy" terms and the public has accepted it as "sin." More recently, however, proponents of gambling have been successful in reframing the argument. Now complex and multidimensional, gambling has developed true advocacy coalitions, and has taken on a more "redistributive" look and feel. An examination of state laws pertaining to gambling helps to demonstrate this point, and that is the focus of the next chapter.

NOTES

1. I previously published much of the material from the Illinois and New Jersey case studies in the October 1998 edition of *Comparative State Plitics*. (The journal no longer exists.)

2. The other five questions and the percent responding "Agree" were as follows: (1) There is a danger of the state becoming too dependent on gambling revenue (49 percent). (2) An increase in lottery sales will also cause more compulsive or problem gambling (48 percent). (3) The lottery encourages poor people who really cannot afford it to gamble and waste their money (51 percent). (4) The lottery is like a hidden tax on the poor because they play more often than the wealthy, and the chances of winning are slim (53 percent). (5) An increase in lottery advertising will cause more people to play (63 percent).

3. For example, in 1983 and 1985, the question was: "In order to raise more money, the state government in Alabama should have a lottery. Do you strongly agree, agree, disagree, or strongly disagree?"

4. While the earlier tables do not include casino gaming on Indian reservations, those facilities now put casino gambling within the reach of so many.

5. Some articles have used other religious membership measures such as percent Baptist or percent Protestants.

6. There are two EHA Models:

Equation One: $Lottery_{i,t}$ F (b_1 Income$_{i,t-1}$ − b_2Fiscal$_{i,t-1}$ − b_3 Religion$_{i,t}$ + b_4Lottery1st$_{i,t}$ − b_6Party$i_{,t}$)

Equation Two: $Casino_{i,t}$ F (b_1 Income$_{i,t-1}$ − b_2Fiscal$_{i,t-1}$ − b_3 Religion$_{i,t}$ + b_4Casino1st$_{i,t}$ − b_6Party$_{i,t}$)

7. The detailed results are included in the Appendixes for anyone who is interested in these results.

8. Because the results obtained for the adoption of lotteries were so similar to those in Berry and Berry (1990), I will not replicate that portion of their research.

4

State Regulation of Gambling

As the gambling case studies and adoption model show, state governments have been key players in both the expansion of various forms of gambling and in the attempts to reframe the gambling issue from one of morality policy to one of economic development and revenue creation. This chapter focuses particularly on the fifth component of the morality policy process model: the strategies employed by various players in the gambling policy debates. Beginning with a look at authorizing legislation, this chapter details the political, legal, and bureaucratic strategies and decisions that have shaped U.S. gambling policy in recent decades.

A COMPARISON OF AUTHORIZING LEGISLATION

Clotfelter and Cook assert in their 1989 book that lottery states have clearly engaged in a pattern of diffusion that includes copying, more or less verbatim, the authorizing legislation used by previous adopters. Once established, the state lotteries have followed similar paths: the state legislates a monopoly for itself, establishes a state agency or public corporation to run the lottery, begins operations with a modest number of relatively simple games, and, due to constant pressure for additional revenues, progressively expands the lottery in size and complexity by adding new games.

A review of the 37 states that currently conduct a statewide lottery generally confirms the assertion that states routinely copy one another's lotteries. Twenty-three of the lotteries are run by independent agencies; the other 14 are mostly located within Departments of Revenue or Finance. Thirty-one of these agencies operate under the same rules as other state agencies; the other six specify that lotteries are not subject to the same employment or civil service rules as employees of other agencies.

State distribution of gross lottery receipts follows a very similar pattern as well: Most states pay out approximately 51 percent in prizes, retaining around 31 percent as administrative and advertising cost, and returning around 18 percent in revenue to the state. While these amounts vary somewhat, the general form is nearly universally observed.

The use of lottery funds is somewhat less consistent. Thirteen states have enacted lotteries to provide funds for education: California, Florida, Georgia, Idaho, Illinois, Michigan, Missouri, Montana, New Hampshire, New Jersey, New York, Ohio, and West Virginia. In 15 other states, lottery revenue is directed toward uses as varied as tourism, parks and recreation, economic development, and construction of public buildings. Colorado targets revenues to environmental protection programs; Pennsylvania gives the money to senior citizens programs; and Massachusetts redistributes lottery revenues to local governments, which amounted to over $500 million in FY 1997 and accounted for three-quarters of the state's aid to cities and towns (National Gambling Impact Study Commission [NGISC], 1999).

Revenues typically grow rapidly after the lottery's introduction, then level off, and often will eventually begin to decline. Most states have introduced new products to the lottery line-up in an effort to counteract this decline. Traditional raffle-type games are coupled with a few simple "scratch-off" games at the beginning. The daily numbers games usually follow, modeled on the illegal numbers games historically present in all major American cities. The advantages to the player of this new, legal game include the ability for him to choose his own "lucky" number, thereby giving him a greater sense of participation (his actual odds of winning remain unaffected, of course, by his choices) and allowing him to determine that day if he has won. Because patrons of illegal numbers games typically play quite frequently—many playing every day—the income that can be generated for the state lottery from its legal numbers game is enormous.

States then introduce "Lotto," the game most closely associated with the lottery in the public mind. According to the 1999 NGISC report on lotteries:

Lotto differs from its counterparts in having enormous jackpots, often reaching into the millions and even tens of millions of dollars. It is also the only form of lottery game played by the public. The tremendous publicity generated by the prizes and by the stories of winners has made the lotto part of the general culture. In recent years, the figures for the top prize have continued to increase as multi-state consortia have been formed with a joint jackpot.

The current apex of lottery development is the various "spin-offs" of other popular forms of gambling, such as video lottery terminals (VLTs), various lottery games with ties to sporting events, and even some products that are remarkably like various casino games.

This review of lottery authorization and regulation seems to deny the existence of much in the way of "policy reinvention" of the type documented by Glick and Hayes (1991). Rather, early in the life cycle of lottery adoptions, a standard set of adoption procedures and regulations was developed, and the "social learning process" postulated for regulatory and distributive types of policy by Walker (1969) appears to have been halted. This appears similar to observed reaction to the diffusion of pre-Roe abortion reform (Mooney & Lee, 1995).

Casino authorizations have been much less consistent than have been lottery authorizations. Among the more obvious differences are the physical and geographical requirements many states have built into their legislation. Other stipulations, such as requiring some riverboat casinos to cruise while gambling takes place and restricting the number and location of operators, provide a wealth of detail about the mind-set of legislators engaged in the legalization of gambling.

Table 4.1 shows the basic differences in authorizing legislation for casinos and related gambling forms. While the majority of states allowing casinos require that gambling take place on some sort of "vessel," others have opted for land-based casinos or card rooms. Several states explicitly state their economic development intentions. For example, Indiana and Iowa inserted sections requiring that hiring preference be granted to local residents.

Table 4.1
State Casino Legislation and Restrictions

State	YR	Type	Location	#Lic.	Form	Tax %
CA	1988	Card rooms	Statewide w/local app.	n/a	Cards	*
CO	1990	Casino	Selected mtn. towns	n/a	Slots, cards	18**
IL	1991	River	Specified	10	Slots,	20
IN	1992	River boats	Specified lake/river	4	Slots, cards, keno	20
IA	1989	River boats	Statewide w/local app	12	Slots, cards	20
LA	1990	River boats	Specified lake/river	15	Any	18.5
		Land-based	New Orleans	1	Any	21
MS	1991	Dock-side	Specified Gulf/MS river	n/a	Any (exc. sports)	8***
MO	1991	River-boats	Specified MS/MO river sites	7	Cards video poker	20
NV	1931	Land-based	Statewide	n/a	Any	6.25
NJ	1976	Land-based	Atlantic City	n/a	Any, (exc. sports)	8
SD	1989	Land-based	Specified towns	n/a	Lim.stakes slots, cards	8

*Only local taxes collected.
**applies to AGR over $5 million (2-15 percent applied to smaller AGR).
***Optional local 4 percent tax is also collected by most counties

Sources: Arthur Andersen (1996); American Gaming Association website: <http://www.americangaming.org/>.

Some of the most obvious differences relate to licensure. For example, among the six states that currently allow some form of riverboat gambling, most limit the number of available licenses in some way. Illinois allows only a set number of licenses; Louisiana provides for no more than six riverboats to operate in any one parish; and Indiana law specifies both the number and location of available licenses.

The original authorizing legislation for riverboat casinos in several of these states included language limiting either the bet or loss limits (Iowa's original law is a particularly stringent example) or limiting the time that ships were allowed to cruise (thereby limiting the time that patrons could gamble). Most of these original restrictions have been either relaxed or entirely repealed.

The tax and fee structures vary somewhat predictably with the general regulatory environment; the more strictly regulated gambling locales tend to impose the highest levels of taxation. The "least" regulated states, especially Mississippi, Nevada, and New Jersey, all have relatively low tax levels. The tax rates range from a low of just 6.25 percent in Nevada to as high as a 35 percent maximum rate in Illinois.

How can the differences be explained? All states impose tax on the gross gaming revenue, or the amount wagered less winnings paid out. Unlike most forms of business taxation, these levies are imposed before any operating expenses are deducted. Thus, the effective rates of taxation are actually much greater than the stated amounts because there are no deductions allowed.

In states with limited licenses, operators are confident that they will be able to achieve a certain market share even with substantially lowered marketing efforts. In those markets without such limitations, casinos must be much more competitive because new entry into the market is not limited. Properties are constantly being upgraded, expanded, and repositioned, as casinos continually try to outdo one another.

Under such a scenario, higher tax rates become a severe disincentive for continued development, and operators will tend to seek an alternative location with either a lower tax rate or a limit on the number of licenses available. Thus, states have essentially had to make an early political choice to allow unfettered casino growth with lower tax rates, or else to restrict the number of licenses (along with the potential non-casino developments associated with the "Las Vegas–style resorts") while extracting a substantially higher rate of tax.

Fully accounting for those differences is not possible at this time, given that only three states (Nevada, New Jersey, Mississippi) currently have a truly open and competitive market. "Open and competitive" can be defined as markets that allow unrestricted licensing of full-scale land-based or permanently moored casinos. Why would unrestricted licensing of floating riverboat casinos or of card rooms not qualify? The answer is that the casino renewing and expanding behaviors are only plausible at the land-based or land-attached casinos. Further, locations allowing only card games have never been able to generate the level of revenue that must be present first if such additional non-gaming development is to occur.

An equally important political decision, as this research has demonstrated, is where and how the gaming tax revenues will be spent. As with state lottery adoptions, casinos have been touted by supporters as a relatively painless way to raise significant amounts of new revenue for states and local governments. Getting political support for that notion has often involved deal making that provides for earmarking of some or all of casino tax revenues to certain sectors to satisfy various political demands.

Most casino states put some portion of casino tax revenues into their general fund. Only the state of Louisiana sends all of those revenues to its general fund without further restriction. Projects ranging from tourism promotion to education and historic preservation to road improvements and disability services are all funded by various states with some portion of their casino tax revenues.

Local governments, as well, tend to receive casino taxes or fees and use them for services related to infrastructure development and/or provision of services to the casino area. In Mississippi, for instance, local governments may use an optional 4 percent tax to help fund educational programs. Local education officials complain that their facilities have been severely stressed with the addition of thousands of new casino employees to the area. Similar scenarios have occurred in other states. Indiana and Iowa both return a portion of their gaming tax revenues to local governments to defray, at least in part, increased costs associated with casino development.

Casino authorizing and regulatory legislation is fertile ground for additional research into the social learning process that is presumed to accompany the diffusion of state policies. Adoption of casinos is still a relatively new phenomenon, and it is clear that consensus as to which form of casino authorization is "best" does not yet exist. States are carefully watching one another's actions and are clearly modifying existing laws pertaining to casinos as the uncertain forces of competition and innovation begin to have an impact.

What is less clear now is whether the learning curve of casino authorizations will become truncated, as has been observed in other morality policies. Casino gambling is a policy realm that can make compromise difficult. In such a situation, advocates on both sides are likely to be forced to seek alternatives: "the courts, direct democracy mechanisms, and so forth" (Mooney & Lee, 1995, p. 621).

Indeed, a four-year-long battle in Mississippi involves ongoing court action and a drive by casino opponents to ban gambling through the state's initiative process. Courts in Arkansas have foiled several attempts to put casino initiatives on the ballot there as well. Casino opponents in Mississippi and supporters in Arkansas have both vowed to continue their efforts.

OTHER STATE ACTIONS RELATING TO GAMBLING

Gaming regulatory agencies, often established initially by persons with solid credentials as "enforcement" or as a "watchdog" over the industry, have, in most states, fairly rapidly altered their stance to become more congenial to, or even promoters of, the industry they are charged with regulating. This squares well with an earlier body of research into the "capture" effects on regulatory bodies (Huntington, 1952; Kolko, 1965; McConnell, 1966). Although more recent evidence discounts the incidence of such capture effects in modern social regulatory agencies (Eisner, 1993; Meier, 1988, pp. 21–25; Worsham, 1997), it appears that they may be alive and well in morality regulation.

An extreme example is the state lottery agency. In the late 1960s and early 1970s, as states first began to operate lotteries, lottery agencies were established to oversee the operation of the games and to ensure that they were conducted fairly (Clotfelter & Cook, 1989). These early lottery agencies were typically headed by officials with backgrounds in law enforcement. As the games became more popular, however, and as more states began to allow lotteries, the need to operate in a competitive environment arose, and the lottery agencies began to be viewed in a new light.

By the early 1980s, close to two dozen state lotteries were running, and state lottery agencies found themselves facing pressure from state legislators to keep lottery revenues high. With greater competition and public awareness of games offered in neighboring states, these agencies recognized a need to offer a broader array of lottery games, and to better promote those new games to the public, in order to meet the revenue demands. Thus state lottery agencies, originally created to police the games, evolved into a quasi-business, quasi-government agency heavily involved in both product design and advertising.

Casino gambling commissions are not immune to these pressures. They, too, were often initially headed by persons with strong law enforcement credentials. In recent years, however, most states have named gaming commissioners with casino industry ties and experience. Gaming commissions in states such as Nevada, Mississippi, Louisiana, New Jersey, Illinois, and, more recently, Michigan have been publicly accused of being "too friendly" with the casinos.

A legislative oversight committee in Mississippi wrote scalding comments in its 1996 review of the state gaming commission: "MGC's [Mississippi Gaming Commission's] failure to regulate Mississippi's legalized gambling industry aggressively and failure to monitor the industry's negative social consequences," result in a perception shared by many that MGC is "too close to the industry"—i.e., that it seeks to protect and promote the industry which it is supposed to regulate (PEER Committee, 1996, p. 47).

Another area of concern—one typical of large, profitable industries—is the "revolving door" between regulators and casinos. Most states stipulate some "cooling-off period," ranging from one to four years, during which time a former gaming regulator or commission member may not seek employment with any of the state's casino firms. The laxity in some states' laws has raised concerns (Pulley, 1998b); however, few states have moved to strengthen these laws.

Many casino states require other mechanisms designed to avoid the appearance of too much state support for the casinos. Nearly all casino states either require a proactive local referendum vote or provide opportunities for communities to say no to casinos through the ballot box. Most have either on occasion or at regular intervals paid for studies of the effects of casinos on local communities, and several require casinos to participate (either directly or through some portion of the taxes they pay) in programs designed to limit and/or treat gambling addiction.

These actions present a very palpable example of how the political processes of regulating gambling have strategically attempted to divorce themselves from the underlying moral questions relating to gambling. At the very least, the persons involved have attempted to appease both public opinion and the various pro-gambling interests. Capture theories contend these interests would indeed arise to defend gambling once it was made legal.

Overall, state adoptions and regulations of gambling have proceeded in a somewhat predictable and desirable pattern. State governments engage in both regulation and control, on the one hand, and promotion in order to maximize revenues, on the other hand. Given the states' unique role in lottery operation, this balancing act is felt most keenly in that area. Casino regulators as well feel the pressure to balance morals with economics, to promote allowable forms of gambling as "entertainment" while severely restricting illegal gambling activities.

THE MISSISSIPPI CASE STUDY OF GAMBLING AUTHORIZATION AND REGULATION

Mississippi has seen the greatest, and the fastest, growth of any of the casino markets opening since 1990. Unlike the majority of states authorizing casinos since 1990, Mississippi has adopted a market-oriented regulatory structure. Simply stated, while most locations limit the number of casino licenses that may be granted, and many place credit, loss, or wager limits on betting, Mississippi has chosen to allow full and open competition among casinos.

The Decision to Adopt Competitive Casino Gambling in Mississippi

On December 19, 1987, the *Europa Star* docked in Biloxi and ushered in a new era of legal gaming in Mississippi that continues to this day. The gambling vessel left Mississippi waters less than a year later, but it brought back into existence an activity that most people thought had disappeared from the state's Gulf Coast in the 1950s.

Gambling existed in Mississippi long before the *Europa Star* and the present-day explosion of huge, multimillion-dollar casinos; however, for much of the state's history, the gambling that was present was illegal, although often purposefully overlooked by law enforcement.

Most of the illegal gambling at the turn of the twentieth century and beyond took place in small, secluded clubs and speakeasies. Many of these were designed to lure tourists who already frequented the Gulf Coast areas because of their scenic beauty and favorable weather. By the 1950s many gaming establishments were well entrenched along the coast, particularly in the Biloxi area (Palermo, 1998).

Politically, these illegal gambling operations were allowed to flourish because the Gulf Coast was considered a "different" part of Mississippi. The area was a summertime getaway for tourists from several nearby states. Political power in the state resided largely in the northern agricultural regions and to a lesser extent in the state capital of Jackson. The casinos were tolerated because they posed no threat to the rest of the state. Biloxi was known statewide as "sin city" (O'Brien, 1998, p. 114).

The illegal gambling was officially shut down when Senator Estes Kefauver held hearings on the Gulf Coast exposing the influence of organized crime at many of the establishments. Many local residents say the illegal casinos never went away completely, but they were certainly forced underground (Palermo, 1998).

The climate for gambling changed again in December 1987 when the *Europa Star* claimed that the waters of the Mississippi Sound were "international" waters and were thus not subject to the jurisdiction of the state of Mississippi. Mississippi lawmakers countered that they could control activities in the Sound, and a lawsuit ensued. The state eventually won their case when the court decided that international waters began beyond the barrier islands in the Gulf of Mexico.

Meanwhile, the state legislature, like its counterpart in Georgia, was considering a state lottery. Ray Mabus, Mississippi's Democratic governor, proposed a lottery as part of an ambitious education reform plan. The voters seemed to approve—state polls showed 62 percent support ("Mississippi," 1990). Yet, behind the scenes, key legislators from the Gulf Coast and the Delta region were coming together with a plan to allow casino riverboat or dockside gambling as a means of both revenue creation and economic development for their beleaguered economies.

The first proposal to legalize dockside gaming in Mississippi was introduced by Democratic State Representative Tommy Walman, whose district would not have been a potential casino site. Walman's proposal would allow dockside casino gambling on the Gulf Coast and along the Mississippi River, but his bill lacked provision for proper regulation and failed to get out of committee. Democratic State Senator Tommy Gollott of Biloxi countered with his own proposal, which included creation of a five-member gaming commission to be housed in the State Tax Commission (Minor, 1989).

In March 1990, each House passed a version of a casino bill, but differences had to be worked out. The lottery amendment proposal was also still very much alive. By the middle of March, both Houses had passed the Gaming Control Act, and the lottery was now facing a new source of opposition: casino-friendly legislators. Governor Mabus pressed on, calling the legislature back into special session in June 1990. The lottery votes eventually came: the House voted 83–39 in favor on June 19, and two days later the Senate voted 28–23. These majorities were not enough. As a constitutional amendment, the lottery vote required a two-thirds majority in each House, and the Senate vote fell far short (King, 1994).

The lottery was not dead—yet. In the spring of 1992, after several counties had already voted to allow casinos and a few others had voted not to do so, the legislature again took up a lottery amendment measure. This time it passed with the required votes, and in November 1992, the state's voters approved the new amendment by 53 percent. Now, state law would require the measure to go back to the legislature again: as a revenue raiser, a lottery needed two-thirds passage.

Meanwhile, casinos were up and running. The Diamond Lady and the Emerald Lady, replicas of 1800s paddle-wheel steamboats, were the first ships to enter the Biloxi channel in mid-July 1992. Joined together and dubbed the Isle of Capri casino, the rather downscale casino was quickly called "pile of debris" by competitors (O'Brien, 1998, p. 114). On August 1, the mayor of Biloxi, Pete Halat, shouted: "*Laissez Les Bon Temps Rouler!*" (Let the Good Times Roll!) as thousands boarded the casino boats. Senator Tommy Gollott was the first to roll the dice, and the first to lose money at a Mississippi casino dice table. Biloxi Port Commission Chairman Joe Creel dropped the first token into a slot machine and lost it (Palermo, 1997, p. A-1).

These early "losses" in no way deterred the growth of casinos in the Magnolia State. In their first three months of operation, Biloxi casinos brought in over $75 million in revenue. Wall Street investors took notice, and by December 1992, Mississippi led the South in new job creation, and the state had five operating casinos. The new casinos, and the jurisdictions that were benefiting from their arrival, joined forces with old lottery foes to put a swift end to the 1993 lottery bill. It never came to the floor for a vote.

Establishing a Regulatory Structure in Mississippi

Within two years of the start of gaming operations, the fully developed authorization for casino "vessels" on defined coastal and Mississippi River (and tributary) waterways had become law. That law also included language that created the Mississippi Gaming Commission, which includes three appointed commissioners who oversee the executive director and his staff of nearly 200 people. Under the director are 13 divisions: legal, public affairs, gaming laboratory (which is responsible for all testing of electronic gaming devices), management information systems, compliance, industry relations, operations/research, enforcement, investigations, intelligence, charitable gaming, accounting, and personnel. The legal and intelligence divisions report to the executive director. The gaming laboratory and compliance divisions report to the deputy executive director, and all other divisions report to the chief of staff, who holds the number-three position at the commission (Mississippi Gaming Commission, 2001).

The MGC adopted two regulations shortly after its creation. The first defines and clarifies the types of vessels that may operate in Mississippi, and the second provides geographical clarity to the Gaming Control Act's rather vague language concerning which waterways are acceptable spots for casino gaming. Regulation numbers one and two, passed in November 1990, state that gaming may take place on vessels that are at least 150 feet in length and have at least a 6-foot draft, are certified by the Coast Guard for carrying 200 or more persons, and are in compliance with all health and safety regulations.

The regulations also stipulate that coastal waterways are permissible sights for such vessels only in those areas lying adjacent to the three most southern counties of the state, which would include the Mississippi Sound, St. Louis Bay, Biloxi Bay, and Pascagoula Bay, but would exclude all the rivers and bayous leading into these bays (Mississippi Gaming Commission, 2001).

No one predicted the explosive growth of casinos in the Magnolia State. As of this writing, there are 30 non-Indian casinos in Mississippi, along with one Indian casino located in Philadelphia. One casino is located in Bay St. Louis, 11 in Biloxi/Gulfport, 2 in Greenville, 1 in Lula, 1 in Natchez, 10 in Robinsonville/Tunica, and 4 in Vicksburg.

More surprising than the growth in the number of Mississippi casinos, however, has been the explosive growth in the size and scope of casino resort operations in the state. Prior to the arrival of the first dockside casino, the Mississippi Gulf Coast had approximately 6,400 hotel rooms with virtually no new hotels under construction. By comparison, today, the Mississippi Gulf Coast has over 15,000 rooms, which represents a 130% increase (von Herrmann, Ingram, & Smith, 2000). Thus, a dramatic increase in restaurants, shopping, and entertainment has resulted.

Elsewhere in the state, casino growth has also created tremendous change. In 1992, Tunica had one motel with 20 rooms. Today, the town has well over 6,000 hotel rooms. According to the Tunica Convention and Visitors Bureau, Tunica County is one of the fastest growing destinations in the nation. It is believed that the addition of a new $21 million convention center will help lure conventions and groups too large for individual properties (Tunica Convention and Visitors Bureau, 1999).

Between 1992 and 1999, casinos in Mississippi spent about $4 billion on various construction projects (von Herrmann, Ingram, & Smith, 2000). The explosive growth has occurred in a regulatory environment that has been widely described as relatively lax. Some critics contend that the MGC is at least partially to blame. The *New York Times* has characterized the regulatory agency in Mississippi as having a "spinning door," noting that a number of key MGC members and staff have left the agency to pursue higher-paying jobs as executives in the casino industry (Pulley, 1998a, p. 1b).

The situation is not unique to Mississippi. However, as the third largest gaming destination in the country, Mississippi is the largest gaming state to have failed to pass a significant "cooling-off period" for its gaming regulators. States such as Nevada, New Jersey, and others require those responsible for regulating the gaming industry to wait from one to four years before going to work for any gaming corporation with operations in their state.

The PEER Committee of the Mississippi Legislature (the state's legislative oversight group) has openly criticized the MGC for what it sees as excessive coziness with the casino industry. In its 1996 report, the PEER Committee notes that "MGC's failure to regulate Mississippi's legalized gambling industry aggressively and failure to monitor the industry's negative social consequences" resulted in a perception shared by many that MGC is "too close to the industry"—i.e., that it seeks to protect and promote the industry that it is supposed to regulate (PEER Committee, 1996, p. 47).

For its part, the MGC strongly denies that it has been "cozy" with the gaming industry. Paul A. Harvey, the MCC's executive director in 1996 when the PEER Committee's report was released, vigorously defended his agency.

Expressing in the official agency response that the MGC was "deeply concerned," Harvey noted that "infrastructure regulation has, to date, cost the Mississippi gaming industry in excess of $800 million." Harvey went on to state that his agency had "taken those actions that we feel will allow the State of Mississippi and its citizens the ability to reap the maximum benefits from the passage of the Gaming Control Act, and do not believe that this action results in a 'cozy' relationship with casinos. In fact, this regulation has been a source of continued animosity between the Commission and non-complying casinos" (PEER Committee, 1996, p. i).

An interesting clause in the state's gaming statute caused a small stir in 1998 and raised issues that threaten to reappear in the near future. The statutes provide that gaming is legal in all qualified counties (those with appropriately "navigable" waterways) unless the voters in the county have not voted to prohibit gaming. Once a casino is docked in a county, either because no election was held due to insufficient support on the required petitions or because a majority of voters agreed to the casino, then no later elections are to be held in that county (Mississippi Gaming Commission, 2001).

In 1997 and 1998, State Ballot Initiatives numbers 12 and 13 were circulated, attempting to pass a constitutional amendment banning gambling and casinos in the state. Both initiatives have been judged by the First Circuit of Hinds County, Mississippi, to be unconstitutional, although the decisions are based primarily on procedural improprieties in the wording of those ballot initiatives. The supporters of those amendments have vowed to continue their attempts to ban gaming from Mississippi (Mason & Nelson, 1999).

The MGC took steps in 1998 that could have the effect of limiting further casino expansion in Mississippi to essentially those areas where it is already approved. The MGC rejected a 1997 proposal for a new casino on the Big Black River in Warren County near Hinds County and has sought clarification on the confusing portion of the law, which defines which waterways make acceptable sights for casinos. As this issue works through the MGC and the legislature, it has cooled interest in several other sights; and major players are now said to be limiting their inquiries primarily to the Gulf Coast and the Mississippi River counties (Branson, 1999).

The balancing act required of gaming regulators extends deeply into the political, economic, and social realms where gambling exists. As gambling continues to grow, it invariably impacts the communities and states in which it is located. How do these economic and social impacts of gambling relate to the ongoing political debates over passage of new forms of gambling or of expanding or restricting access to gambling? These questions are addressed in the next chapter.

5

The Economic and Social Impacts of Gambling and Their Effects on Policy

"The Mississippi Miracle" is the way Mississippi's Department of Economic Development has described what has happened to the State's economy since the advent of gaming. A frequent critic of the industry referred to casino developments as "dreamfield delusions" (Grinols & Omorov, 1996). No less a neutral and dispassionate observer than the National Opinion Research Center (NORC) at the University of Chicago has drawn the conclusion that "[t]he net picture in the economic and social impacts data is on the positive side, but not in an overwhelming way." NORC researchers added, "There appears to be more of a shift in the types and locations of work, and perhaps the overall number of workers, than a rise in per capita earnings" (NORC, 1999).

When it comes to determining the economic and social impacts of gambling on communities, the evidence is in, but the jury is still out.

ECONOMIC AND SOCIAL IMPACTS RESEARCH

There is much anecdotal evidence to support the notion that gambling, and particularly casino resort gambling, provides economic benefits for the communities that allow it. In such communities, there is frequently a mountain of economic activity data collected and made available to the public. It should be a simple task to determine whether gambling, indeed, provides more in the way of economic benefit to a given community than it creates in new costs. It should be, but it is not.

Trying to understand why gambling is difficult to analyze in terms of its economic impacts requires some clearheaded thinking that is often lacking in the popular works, and occasionally is lacking in the scholarly research on the subject. Unwittingly, research about casino gaming often begins with a clear bias either for or against gambling. Such biases tend to pervade the research—from what data are collected to how data are analyzed—and so it is that dramatically different conclusions can be drawn from essentially the same set of observable cases. Putting it more plainly: Researchers who look for a particular effect are more likely to find it.

Bias on the part of researchers is not the only potential cause of confusion in the economic impact question. Particularly with respect to casinos and their impact, much of the relevant data are muddled because of the time frame during which the current gambling proliferation has occurred. Many of the states currently offering some form of casino gambling authorized that activity between 1990 and 1992. The national economy at that time was in recession, but quickly began the strong and long-lasting recovery that characterized the decade of the 1990s and beyond. The problem for gaming researchers, then, is how to tease apart the effects of the gambling and its associated economic development activity from the recovery and its general impact. Nearly all of the published studies, including those prepared by several state agencies in gaming states, which we will look at shortly, failed to adequately account for these facts.

The National Gambling Impact Study Commission

Eugene M. Christiansen, a contributor to the final National Gambling Impact Study Commission (NGISC) report, owns and operates a private consulting firm that prepares annual reports on the status and size of the gaming market. In 1998, according to Christiansen, consumers spent about $54 billion on legal commercial games including casinos, lotteries, and pari-mutuels. That $54 billion is more than American consumers spent on movie tickets, spectator sports, cruise ships, video games, recorded music, and theme park attendance, combined (Christiansen, 1999).

Of that $54 billion, about $18.5 billion was paid out to state and local governments in the form of taxes. Clearly, the government revenues generated by gambling are substantial, although they pale in comparison to total sales or personal income taxes collected. When taken in conjunction with the federal income taxes paid on gambling winnings and the income taxes paid by the industry's approximately 600,000[1] employees, it becomes clear that the economic muscle of the gaming industry can scarcely be ignored by state or local government officials. They certainly are not ignoring the industry. Rather, nearly every state in the latter half of the 1990s has authorized and funded some form of gambling impact study (recall that only Hawaii, Tennessee, and Utah allow no legal gambling for non-charitable purposes).

In 1999, Adam Rose, an economist at the University of Pennsylvania, presented his findings, part of the NGISC's report, to Congress. Rose conducted a massive review of existing local, state, and national studies of the economic impacts of gambling. Of the more than 100 studies reviewed, the overwhelming majority were either seriously (and obviously) biased, contained serious methodological flaws and oversights, or both. The study's author then combined the 36 most credible studies into a meta-analysis of the impact of gambling (NGISC, 1999).

Meta-analysis is gaining favor among social scientists because it combines the findings of many independent analyses into one statistical model. Not without its flaws, meta-analysis is, nevertheless, an increasingly acceptable way to "separate the wheat from the chaff," as it were, in policy studies. The combined analysis regresses total gross output in the selected economies on a set of explanatory variables including direct output, casino type, offset effects (which combines both substitution and recapture), and a summary measure for the reliability of the individual studies. The model explains 96 percent of the variance in total output, and estimates a multiplier of 1.81 (NGISC, 1999).

The NGISC findings suggest that for every $1 increase in direct output of the gambling industry, total output in the region rises by $1.81. Overall, the study found that the net impacts of gambling on the U.S. economy have been positive. It is important to understand the limitations of this research, however.

Because direct output of the gambling industry, and imputed multiplier effects from standard input-output or similar economic models were used by nearly all of the studies Rose included, the meta-analysis appears to do little more than confirm the similarity of the earlier findings. What it cannot properly do is determine to what extent the included studies were accurate reflections of gambling's independent impacts on state and local economies. To be fair, the NGISC directive to Professor Rose was to conduct a review of existing studies only—not to conduct original research. His report accomplishes its mission fully.

The study also included an extensive review of the past year and lifetime prevalence of both problem and pathological gambling in the United States. The research team used a combined approach with both a random-digit-dialed telephone survey and patron intercept surveys at various gambling locales. Their basic strategy was to compare rates (and costs) of specific adverse consequences associated with problem and pathological gambling for each designated gambling type.

Problem and pathological gamblers, for example (and perhaps those considered at risk for problem gambling as well), are believed to experience higher rates of personal bankruptcy (primarily attributed to their problems with gambling) than persons who are otherwise similar but do not gamble or are lower risk gamblers. Obviously, there are reasons unrelated to gambling for individuals to experience bankruptcy.

The NGISC analysis examines the following questions:

1. To what extent did the problem and pathological gamblers surveyed experience a certain consequence?
2. To what extent did they attribute the consequence to their gambling?
3. What plausible economic costs can be associated with higher-than-expected rates of this consequence?

As a side issue, the study also was able to confirm earlier research showing that problem gambling cuts across all socioeconomic and racial lines.

Based on these questions, the study concluded that:

1. Problem and pathological gamblers have significantly higher rates of costly consequences than otherwise similar persons do.
2. Problem and pathological gamblers experience or impose thousands of dollars of economic costs per year on society.

3. Problem and pathological gamblers rarely directly attributed these costly
   problems to their gambling behaviors or difficulties.

The bankruptcy cost attributed to problem and pathological gambling, as one example of problem gambling costs, was adjusted for "expected" rates of bankruptcy. Thus, the estimates are of "excessive" costs (be it for bankruptcy, job loss, health problems, and so on) incurred by problem and pathological gamblers.

In attempting to assess social impacts, the study included a survey incorporating questions that explicitly examined behaviors and problems that prior research suggested is disproportionately experienced by this problem and pathological gambling population. The authors estimated that some 3 million Americans have been pathological gamblers at some time in their lives. Their research also shows that about 15 percent of all gambling industry revenues are generated by pathological gamblers, and that each of these individuals costs society $12,000 over his lifetime. Interestingly, most of these gamblers' problems manifest themselves in repeated visits to gambling sites. Since residents are much more likely to visit casinos or play state lotteries frequently than are nonresidents, this suggests that these gambling venues pose a greater problem for residents than for nonresident (and therefore less frequent) visitors.

The NGISC also conducted two reviews of the relationship between crime and gambling, and the findings of both reports can best be summarized as "inconclusive." Part of the research found clear relationships between pathological gamblers and criminal activity; a second portion found little evidence of any causal relationship between the advent of casinos in a community and the rates of a variety of types of crime (NGISC, 1999).

Other National and Statewide Gambling Impact Studies

Ricardo Gazel, an economist with the Federal Reserve Bank in Kansas City, shows clearly and concisely what areas a straightforward, yet thorough, examination of the gambling industry's impacts should include (Gazel, 1998). He argues that much of the published research to date has been done at the behest of the gambling industry itself (echoing the assertion by the NGISC) and thus it tends to examine only the direct positive economic impacts (including such items as

job creation, revenue generation, new construction, and so on). Gazel's 1998 gaming impact design is noteworthy because it includes
discussion of purely economic negative impacts, such as substitution
effects and required increases in various public sector expenditures,
which many of the previous studies tended to ignore. Gazel does
address the social costs, calling them "negative externalities," and includes such items as increased costs of police, corrections, and protection of personal property (Gazel, 1998, p. 72).

While a few recent studies by various states have tried to examine
both positive and negative sides of the industry, they have tended to
focus on the so-called social costs, such as those associated with compulsive gamblers and increased criminal activity. A 1998 report from
the state auditor of Mississippi is typical of many of these state impact
studies. It includes first a general history of the state's experience with
gambling. It then reviews the structure of regulations and tax laws
pertaining to gambling; details the sources of direct revenues received
from the industry; looks at sales taxes, employment, and incomes;
and provides a somewhat cursory review of the social costs of problem
gambling and bankruptcies (Bryant, 1998).

A study of both the social and economic effects of limited stakes
casinos in South Dakota used time series analysis of both benefits and
costs. This research examined trends in transfer payments, child abuse
and neglect cases, bankruptcies, and similar social measures in addition to standard economic performance data such as sales tax collections, property values, and so forth (Madden, 1991). The study
suffers methodologically from the lack of external control variables
that could consider the impact of an expanding economy or similar
factors.

A 1998 study of the economic impacts of casino gaming in Iowa
was publicly criticized for its failure to include the costs of casinos in
the same report which showed that over 86 percent of the money
spent by Iowa casinos stays within the state, and that casinos have an
overall impact of $570 million ("$570 Million Impact," 1998).

The economic impact of Missouri's riverboat casinos was studied
in 1998. A thorough and detailed input-output model was designed
to include direct, indirect, and induced effects of casino gambling.
The estimates included decreases in spending consistent with the notion of cannibalization, or the theory that money spent in casinos is
money "lost" to other local retailers and industries (Leven, Phares,
& Louishomme, 1998).

The Missouri study also notes that casinos probably have higher multiplier effects than many alternative industries, because they are an extremely labor-intensive business. Retailers or restaurants, by contrast, employ large numbers of local people but sell products that, for the most part, are "imports" to the local economy. Multiplier models assume that the higher the proportion of "local" products and people engaged by an industry, the greater would be the impact on the economy (Leven, Phares, & Louishomme, 1998).

The Louisiana Gaming Control Board commissioned a statewide study by the University of New Orleans. Released in 1999, the report used an expansive economic cost-benefit model to determine the impacts of the various forms of legal gambling in that state (Ryan & Speyrer, 1999). The study examined the level of visitors versus residents who gamble, the effects of the industry on crime and certain social problems, and expenditures both in- and out-of-state by the industry.

The research team concluded that riverboat gambling, particularly, provided helpful economic benefits because it provided a way to plug various economic "leaks" from domestic tourist dollars flowing out to other gambling sites. Further, additional benefits were derived from the industry's ability to bring new tourist dollars to the state and thus encourage development in related industries such as retail, restaurants, transportation, and hotels. Costs to the state were found to include losses in productivity, theft, bad debt, and increased criminal justice costs (Ryan and Speyrer, 1999). The study authors cautioned that they were unable to calculate costs of certain other perceived social costs such as possible increases in addictive behaviors, divorce, or suicide.

A 1996 prevalence study conducted for the state of Mississippi (Volberg, 1996), for example, was an important step in understanding the impact of problem gamblers in a state with recently legalized casinos generally. Further, it provides information about the added impact that the legalization of casinos may have had in that state. The study shows that nearly 5 percent of Mississippi residents can be classified as "problem" gamblers. As much as 2 percent of residents have problems severe enough to label them as "probable pathological" gamblers (Volberg, 1996). These numbers are in line with national estimates—meaning that Mississippi does not show a significantly higher prevalence than most other states (those with and those without casinos).

The Mississippi prevalence study also reveals important facts about the demographics of problem versus nonproblem gamblers and the gambling habits of the two groups. To summarize those findings briefly, problem gamblers in Mississippi spend three-and-a-half times, on average, the amount each month for gambling that nonproblem gamblers spend. Some 80 percent of all reported monthly expenditures for gambling by the study group could be accounted for by a very small subset of so-called heavy-spending problem gamblers.[2] The study found that 47 percent of all problem gamblers in Mississippi fall into that heavy-spending group. Problem gamblers often engage heavily in various illegal forms of betting (either in place of or in addition to their participation in legal gambling); this fact was not sorted out in relation to the gamblers' in-casino expenditures.

Problem gamblers in Mississippi are generally younger, more likely to be African American, and more likely to be either divorced or single (as opposed to married) than their counterparts who gamble but do not experience "problem" gambling. What the 1996 prevalence study does not alone reveal is that the impacts from these problem gamblers are likely not evenly distributed across the state. A demographic profile of casino gamblers conducted for the state in 1999 (von Herrmann, Ingram, & Smith, 2000) shows that Mississippi residents are much more likely to gamble in the state's South River area (77 percent) or on the Gulf Coast (39 percent) than in the North River casinos (11 percent).

A 1996 study in Wisconsin provides one of the best examples of an attempt to quantify the effects of problem gamblers in an American state (Thompson, Gazel, & Rickman, 1996). The researchers looked at employment costs, bad debts, civil court costs, thefts, criminal justice costs, therapy costs, and welfare costs.[3] Total annual estimated cost-per-problem gambler in Wisconsin casinos[4] was $10,113. It is noteworthy that only gamblers who were in treatment were included, and thus these estimates are likely significantly higher than would be actual costs for all persons, since it is often serious (and costly) consequences such as arrest or bankruptcy that cause a person to seek treatment.

A review of the Wisconsin study, though, claims that many of the assumptions underlying the research may have caused it to create overly high estimates of social costs. The Wisconsin study included figures for so-called bad debts, for example, but Walker and Barnett (1999) have said those costs are merely transfers—a redistribution of wealth from the creditor to the debtor. Likewise, the category of theft must be excluded, they argue, because it, too, is merely a transfer of existing property from one owner to another. However, if one takes this line of reasoning to its logical conclusion, he would have to conclude that society has no compelling interest in stopping bad debts or thefts of property. Yet, society has such an interest and has repeatedly asserted it via the criminal and civil code.

The series of studies in Wisconsin were conducted to estimate the economic and social effects of Indian casinos there. These studies found that, on balance, the casinos' collective economic impact on the state is positive. Through increases in employment, income tax, sales tax, property tax, and the like, the Wisconsin casinos have generated substantial economic expansion and development (Thompson, Gazel, & Rickman, 1996). The authors found little support for a clear cannibalization effect.[5]

Several states have commissioned studies to determine the economic and/or social impact of potential or proposed casino gambling on their states. One Kentucky report found that the state's residents spent about $1 billion on gambling trips outside the state in 1998. Most of that amount was for food, lodging, and transportation. Gambling losses were $433 million, nearly half of which was dropped at riverboat casinos just over the Kentucky state line, the report said. It went on to say that Kentucky could capture a big chunk of that money by expanding its own gambling, especially with casinos or with racetrack "wagering parlors" equipped with slot machines and video lottery terminals. The report also said the social costs—divorce, family deprivation, and the like—could only be speculated. The report by PricewaterhouseCoopers, a national accounting and consulting firm, was commissioned after Kentucky's governor floated the idea of creating casinos to raise money for the horse industry, for cities, and for the preservation of farmland and natural areas ("Kentucky Gambling Study," 1999).

The California Research Bureau was commissioned to perform an analysis of gambling for the Golden State. The finished product was essentially a review of existing publications relating to economic, social, and other benefits and costs of gambling. While extremely thorough, the California study provides little in the way of new information. However, this study is unique among the state reports in that it pays some attention to the notion of consumer surplus, which is essentially the difference between what a consumer is willing, or expects, to pay for something and the actual price charged. The author of the California study implies that some communities may be quite willing to pay higher costs in exchange for the benefits that casinos can bring (Dunstan, 1997).

A thorough and complex study prepared in Florida found that expenditure substitutions and leakages, as well as the imputed costs arising from various social impacts, would offset much of the economic benefit to be derived from casino gambling there (Florida Office of Planning and Budgeting, 1992).

A 1996 report on the economic development potential and impacts of casinos in Indiana, done by Purdue economist David Broomhall, makes an important contribution to the body of economic impacts literature by clearly delineating the requirements that must be met if casinos are to provide true economic development. The report states

For legalized gambling to create economic development it must do two things: provide a positive economic contribution to the economy and draw clientele from outside the local economy. The measure of a positive economic contribution to the economy is somewhat subjective, but it means the expansion and diversification of the economic base, the generation of jobs that pay reasonable wages, and improvements in public and private services such as cultural amenities, restaurants, and shopping. Generally speaking, the jobs created, both directly by the gambling operation and indirectly, should be of at least similar quality and average wage as the existing employment base. (p. 2)

Broomhall concludes that by limiting the number of licenses and by authorizing casinos in an area where competing casino facilities already exist in nearby states Indiana effectively limited the potential economic impact that its riverboat casinos could have, while potentially increasing certain social impacts.

One of the better known experts in the field of problem gambling and its impacts is Henry Lesieur. The author of several books and dozens of articles on the subject, Lesieur wrote that some forms of gambling pose a much greater threat to those with gambling problems than do others. He found that problem gamblers account for much larger portions of revenue generated by video gambling, table games, horses, and bingo than by other gambling forms such as slots, lotto, and instant lottery games (Lesieur, 1984). Overall, he estimates that problem gamblers account for anywhere from 23 percent to 41 percent of all gaming revenues (Lesieur, 1998).

The vast majority of studies of problem and pathological gamblers have not been conducted at the national level but, rather, in specific states or localities. Further, much of this research (like Lesieur's) is international, focusing on gamblers in a variety of countries that operate a wide array of gambling forms. While these studies are too numerous to review in this chapter, several excellent reviews of existing literature on the subject have already been prepared.[6]

In broad terms, the research concludes that problem and pathological gambling has serious economic and social consequences. This small number of gamblers creates large, often unrecoverable debts (Thompson, Gazel, & Rickman, 1996). They experience increased levels of marital problems (Lorenz & Yaffee, 1987), a variety of medical problems (Lorenz & Yaffee, 1986), and are involved in various illegal activities (Lesieur, 1984; Thompson, Gazel, & Rickman, 1995).

THEORIES OF HOW ECONOMIC AND SOCIAL IMPACTS RELATE TO GAMBLING POLITICS

What do the various economic and social impact studies have to say about the morality politics model and how well it fits in the area of gambling policy? More important, does the model provide a framework that can be used to explain the impacts of gambling and how those impacts will be interpreted and pulled into the ongoing political debates about gambling policy?

The history of gambling in the United States, as noted earlier, includes a period of openly corrupt, mostly private gambling enterprises, followed by a rather long period of outright prohibition, followed by the current period of renewed legal gambling activity under fairly tightly controlled circumstances. Because of concerns about gambling and its historic ties to criminality and corruption, most states have sought either to run a state monopoly gambling enterprise (e.g., a state lottery) or to create either monopoly or oligopoly gambling in a limited geographic region.

The result, in terms of economic impact, is that limited gambling can have only limited direct effect on state and local economies. Further, as much of the research just detailed demonstrates, such limited gambling (particularly in the form of riverboat casino gambling) creates little in the way of general non-gambling development and likely results in a far greater amount of both economic substitution effects and what Gazel (1998) called the "negative externalities." Thus, in a very palpable way, the history of the gambling industry continues to shape its bottom line.

If one were to consider personal and ethical impacts of gambling in an attempt to determine social impacts, the scope and number of studies to be reviewed would be enormous. As I have shown, much of this research into the social impacts of gambling in the United States focuses attention on a small group (national estimates place it at around 3–5 percent) of the population whose gambling creates major negative effects in their lives. These problem and pathological gamblers are expected to be at the root of many of the social ills associated with gambling, since by definition their gambling goes beyond the limits of mere recreation.

The presence of a state lottery or of land, riverboat, or dockside casinos arguably presents some risk to the communities in which they are located and to the whole state as well. The economic impact research I have reviewed here suggests that political elites and the gambling industry might be responsible for the spread of gambling. Other evidence, such as that in the 1999 national study (NGISC, 1999), hints that the public may simply be more interested in gambling now than it was in the past. At least three competing (but also potentially complementary) hypotheses can be asserted, then, about who and what is driving the implementation and reformulation of gambling policy.[7]

1. *Gambling regulation, and discussion of its social impacts, is a function of the value-based and economically based opinions of persons who oppose or support gambling.* The current demand for gambling is high. Depending on the form of gambling under consideration, as much as 80 percent of the population is interested in at least occasional participation. Yet, as this chapter will show, survey research conducted at both the state and national level over two decades shows that, consistently, the American public worries about the potential social costs of gambling.

2. *Gambling regulation and social impacts discussion are a function of industry preferences, or of the preferences of special interest groups opposed to gambling.* As gaming grew and spread through the 1990s, corporations that owned and operated casinos were motivated to protect the public image of their industry and to appear to be proactive about possible

negative social impacts. The industry has worked hard to win, from various state regulators, the ability to self-police in the area of dealing with problem gaming, and that has had important impacts on policy.

3. *Gambling regulation and social impacts discussion are a function of the preferences of political elites and elected officials who seek to maximize the benefits to themselves or to their constituencies.* For many years, political scientists have been interested in the learning and decision processes that drive elites and elected officials to enact certain legislation while opposing other laws. The state case studies presented earlier suggest that competitive and diffusion pressures are likely at work in the spread of legal lotteries and casinos.

Politicians likely have other reasons for supporting gambling: to provide increased revenues without general tax increases, for example, or to provide economic stimulus and tourism development without the need for costly development incentives from the state or local government. Likewise, those opposing gambling have important reasons to discuss it in ways which, as Meier would predict, allow "worst-case scenarios" to dominate in a situation in which the rarity of the effects in question matters not (Meier, 2001, p. 33).

In order to compare these various approaches to the economic and social impacts questions, I will examine public opinion data, several gambling industry reports, and public comments from a variety of political leaders.

Public Opinion Data on Support for Gambling

Several national polling organizations have asked questions about gambling. An April 1989 CBS News–*New York Times* (CBS/*NYT*) poll asked a dozen questions about gambling, including questions about support for gambling policy and respondents' own gambling activities. One reason why this poll is useful to the present study is that it was conducted in 1989, a year that marked a "crest" in the current wave of gambling policy adoptions.

Using stratified random digit dialing, the poll sampled 1,412 adults aged 18 and over. Respondents were asked a series of questions on gambling, including whether they approved of state lotteries, casinos, off-track-betting parlors, and sports betting. In addition, respondents' party affiliation, ideological preference, age, income, gender, religious preference, educational attainment level, and race were asked. Pollsters also included information about the size and character of place in which respondents reside (urban, central city, suburb), and whether the respondent is from a lottery state.

Another poll, conducted in 1992 by Gallup for *USA Today*, asked mostly questions about approval or disapproval of five common forms of gambling. The Gallup poll used a stratified telephone sample of 1,200 adults aged 18 and over. It asked about their attitudes regarding gambling policy and their own gambling behaviors, as well as demographic information similar to the CBS poll.

A third nationwide poll was conducted one year later. This poll was conducted on September 13–15, 1993, by Gallup for CNN/*USA Today*; it surveyed 1,400 respondents on both their views regarding gambling and their personal gambling activities. That poll did not ask questions about support for various forms of gambling, but instead surveyed people's general feelings regarding gambling and how frequently they gamble.

Simple frequency distributions, conducted on the 1989 CBS national poll data, reveal that, in general, support for gambling is high, with lotteries receiving the greatest level of approval. Of the 1,412 respondents, 1,099, or 77 percent, said they approve of state lotteries, 55 percent approved of casinos, and 49 percent approved of off-track betting.

The 1992 *USA Today* poll finds essentially the same results as the CBS poll. Both polls show substantially higher support for state lotteries than for any other form of legalized gambling. Table 5.1, which summarizes these findings, also reveals that overall most Americans favor most forms of legalized gambling, with the exception of betting on professional sports, which fails to achieve a majority in either survey.

Another national poll is conducted annually for the Harrah's Entertainment Corporation, Inc. The 1999 poll, and several earlier polls conducted for Harrah's, showed that roughly 60 percent of the adult population in the United States considers gambling an acceptable activity for anyone. Another 30 percent were of the opinion that gambling is not acceptable for them, but conceded that it might be all right for others; another 10 percent believe gambling is unacceptable for anyone (Harrahs, 1999).

The 1993 CNN/*USA Today* poll asks a question that is particularly helpful in determining who tends to support gambling in general. While most poll questions ask about support for specific forms of

Table 5.1
National Support for Various Forms of Gambling, 1989–1992

CBS/NYT, 1989
Q: "As you may know, some states legalize betting so that the state can raise revenues. Please tell me whether you approve or disapprove of legalizing each of the following types of betting in your state to help raise revenues (If already legal ask, do you approve of its being legal?)"

	Approve	Disapprove	Don't Know
Lotteries for cash prizes	77%	19%	4%
Casino gambling at resort areas	55	45	5
Off-track betting on horse races	49	44	7
Betting on professional sports events such as baseball, basketball, or football?	43	52	5

Gallup/USA Today, 1992
Q: "Please tell me whether you would approve or disapprove of legalizing each of the following types of betting in your state to help raise revenues . . . ?

	Approve	Disapprove	Don't Know
Lotteries for cash prizes	75%	21%	4%
Casino gambling on riverboats	60	35	5
Casino gambling at resort areas	51	40	9
Betting on professional sports	33	64	3

Source: CBS/*NYT* poll of 1,412 U.S. residents, conducted April 13–16, 1989; Gallup/*USA Today* poll of 1,200 U.S. residents, conducted April 2, 1992.

gambling such as the lottery, casinos, or pari-mutuels, this poll included a question about whether gambling itself is a moral or immoral activity.[8]

Hugick and Saad conducted cross-tabulations on the responses and various demographic factors. They found that support for gambling comes more from those under the age of 60, those with higher education, those with higher incomes, non-Southerners, those who do not attend church, Catholics, and Liberals, although support is high among all groups (Hugick & Saad, 1994, p. 13). Using the same technique on the 1989 CBS/*NYT* poll data reveals that many of the basic patterns of support for lotteries emerge again. The results, shown in Table 5.2, include information about urban versus rural

Table 5.2
Cross-Tabulations on Support for Lottery and
Demographic Variables in a National Survey, 1989

	Variable	% Supporting ♦
Race:	Whites	80.8%
	Blacks	81.0%
	Chi-Square:	1.396
Educ:	H.S. or less	67.1%
	More Than H.S.	82.4%
	Chi-Square:	22.625**
Age:	18–40	86.4%
	41–60	78.1%
	61+	69.4%
	Chi-Square:	39.271**
Inc:	Less than $12K	70.8%
	$12–$25K	78.8%
	$25–$35K	82.4%
	$35–$50K	83.0%
	Over $50K	85.7%
	Chi-Square:	16.425**
	Variable	% Supporting
Urban:	Urban area	83.9%
	Suburb	81.5%
	Small towns	75.7%
	Rural area	76.4%
	Chi-Square:	8.872*

** = significant at the .01 level
* = significant at the .05 level
♦—Question wording appears in Table 6.1

Source: CBS/*NYT* Poll of 1,412 U.S. residents, conducted April
13–16, 1989.

dwellers, a category that was not examined in the CNN/*USA Today*
survey. Support for state lotteries is again highest among the young,
those with middle to upper personal income levels, higher than a high
school education, and urban dwellers. The race variable did not produce significant results in the cross-tabulation analysis.

But what of support for other forms of gambling? Do the same demographic and social factors tend to vary with support for casinos, off-track betting, or sports betting? In order to arrive at some conclusions, additional cross-tabulations, using the same national survey, are conducted.

The results, shown together in Table 5.3, illustrate first that support for all forms of gambling tends to come from persons within similar demographic groups. For example, the young again emerge as some of the strongest supporters of all forms of gambling, an influence most notable in support for legalized betting on sports. Across all forms of gambling examined, support declines as respondents' age increases.

Along other demographic lines, support for sports betting reacts differently than support for lotteries, casinos, and off-track betting—for example, those with less than a high school education were more likely to support sports betting than those with more education. Neither the race nor the income variables was significant for either casinos or sports betting, and the race variable was also not significant for off-track betting.

Party identification, ideology, and religious affiliation and participation were also examined. As Table 5.4 reveals, for all forms of gambling except sports betting, variables for liberal ideology, Catholic Church membership, and infrequent attendance at church services were most likely to point to support for gambling.

Persons calling themselves "Independents" are slightly more likely to support lotteries than partisans. Opinions regarding betting on sports again conform to a different pattern than do opinions on other forms of gambling; those who say they rarely or never attend church are much less likely to support such proposals than their counterparts who attend services frequently. These data suggest that voters may view legalized betting on sports as a very different policy than other forms of gambling. Yet when data on other forms of gambling are examined, the pattern that emerges is a fairly consistent one: support is greatest among the young, those with more than a high school education, urban residents, those with middle to upper incomes, liberals, Catholics, and those who attend church services infrequently.

Support for Gambling in Statewide Poll Data

It is difficult to make cross-state comparisons about public opinion, even though certain questions are repeated in identical, or very nearly

Table 5.3
**Cross-Tabulations on Support for Other Gambling and Demographic
Variables in a National Survey, 1989**

		Percent Supporting*		
Variable		Casinos	OTB	Sports
Race:	Whites	57.2%	52.5%	55.5%
	Blacks	59.0%	56.6%	50.0%
	Chi-Sq:	0.222	0.593	1.910
Educ:	H.S. or less	47.6%	41.9%	62.3%
	More Than H.S.	58.6%	54.4%	53.7%
	Chi-Sq:	7.245*	9.093**	4.331*
Age:	18–40	62.4%	57.0%	52.9%
	41–60	57.3%	52.7%	44.6%
	61+	44.4%	42.3%	27.2%
	Chi-Sq:	26.867**	17.018**	53.559**
Inc:	Less than $12K	50.6%	38.9%	58.9%
	$12–$25K	55.5%	51.0%	58.3%
	$25–$35K	58.6%	57.0%	52.3%
	$35–$50K	57.4%	55.3%	53.5%
	Over $50K	63.2%	57.0%	51.5%
	Chi-Sq:	7.024	16.834**	4.800
Urban:	Urban area	65.1%	66.1%	48.6%
	Suburb	61.8%	55.9%	52.7%
	Small towns	57.1%	47.8%	52.1%
	Rural area	50.2%	44.9%	61.5%
	Chi-Sq:	14.738**	20.441**	11.242*

* = significant at the .05 level
** = significant at the .01 level
Please note: Question wording appears in Table 5.1.

Source: CBS/*NYT* Poll of 1,412 U.S. residents, conducted April 13–16, 1989.

identical, form by numerous state polling organizations. They are typically, although not always, located within major state universities or at major statewide newspapers and, thus, are difficult to find. No single organization polls an appropriately sized sample of residents in each state in order to determine each state's level of approval for any specific policy item.

Table 5.4
Cross-Tabulations on Support for Gambling and Certain Variables in a National Survey, 1989

Variable		Lott	Percent Supporting Casinos	OTB	Sports
Party	Dem	81.1	57.4	53.7	54.6
	Rep	77.4	54.2	49.6	60.3
	Ind	85.0	61.3	56.6	47.5
	Chi-Sq:	7.845*	4.188	4.186	13.74*
Ideology	Lib	89.0	69.2	62.3	44.7
	Mod	75.1	51.6	48.3	60.1
	Cons	83.4	58.8	54.2	54.2
	Chi-Sq:	24.47**	22.48**	13.54**	16.58*
Religion	Cath	89.7	67.8	61.4	49.3
	Prot	77.4	53.7	49.9	56.6
	Ch-Sq:	24.38**	20.33**	12.99**	5.54
Attend_Ch	Every Wk	63.2	38.5	35.4	71.6
	Weekly	80.1	50.6	45.7	59.5
	2 × Mo	82.9	62.3	59.3	50.0
	2 × Yr	92.0	67.8	62.2	45.1
	Never	91.0	76.1	69.1	39.3
	Ch-Sq:	129.22**	111.09**	58.94**	83.51*

Notes: Question wording appears in Table 5.1.
* = significant at the .05 level
** = significant at the .01 level

Source: CBS/*NYT* Poll of 1,412 U.S. residents, conducted April 13–16, 1989.

The situation is further complicated because these state poll results are not always presented in a clear or complete fashion. The *American Public Opinion Index* for the period 1989 to 1993 includes listings for questions about lotteries, gambling, and casinos (the time frame is designed to be relatively close to the recent significant debates on the subject, as well as to the national sample). Other surveys are listed in indexes published by various larger city news organizations (such as the *Chicago Tribune* and the *New York Times*). In all, a search of these volumes turned up 32 different state survey questions regarding opinions on gambling policy conducted during the period 1988–

1993. The states, years, polling organizations, and questions are summarized in Table 5.5.

The prospective lottery questions were asked predominantly in Southern states, including Alabama, Louisiana, Mississippi, North Carolina, Tennessee, and Texas. In addition, 13 questions about support of proposed casinos were asked, but unlike the lottery questions, these were asked by surveys in states throughout the United States. Three questions about support of proposed pari-mutuel or other gambling at current betting facilities were asked in Alabama, Georgia, and Missouri.

In these statewide polls, support for the various forms of gambling closely resembles the national poll data described earlier, with only a few notable exceptions. Overall, in states where questions about state lotteries are asked, public support for them appears high. Among the 15 state polls asking questions about lotteries, none found less than majority support; and in several of these state polls, support was found to be above 65 percent. Iowa, Nevada, and Texas respondents were supportive of lotteries in these polls; each of these surveys found 70 percent supporting a state lottery.

Casinos fared less well overall than lotteries. Respondents in 10 of the 13 states where questions concerning proposed casinos were asked did not support these proposals by a majority. Only Alabama, Louisiana, and New Jersey residents expressed support for proposed casinos in various locations in their state. It is interesting to note that 66 percent of New Jersey respondents also agreed that the existing casinos in that state had been "a good thing." Support for casinos was below 40 percent in Georgia, Illinois, and West Virginia.

Obviously, the difficulty with this data set is that only 24 states are covered by any of these poll results. There is no information about how residents of other states felt about various gambling proposals during the same time frame. Another problem lies in the slight variations in the wording of the questions, which could be troublesome if such questions were to be analyzed comparatively.

Why Do People Support or Oppose Gambling?

Both the national and state survey data I have discussed suggest that the public views different gambling policies differently. The CBS/*NYT* poll done in 1989 reveals that 40 percent of all respondents had never personally gambled, even though many of them said

Table 5.5
A Sampling of Available State Survey Data

	Year	% Positive	State	Poll
Lottery Questions				
"Do you Support[1] or				
Oppose a Lottery?"	1988	65.8	AL	SOR
	1989	62.0	NC	CP
	1989	64.0	TN	SSRI
	1989	67.9	TX	TP
	1989	64.0	WY	UW
	1990	67.0	LA	TIMES–P
	1990	65.8	MS	MS
	1990	70.0	NV	CAR
	1991	70.0	TX	TP
"Should the State	1990	65.8	AL	CAP
have a lottery?"	1993	66.8	AL	SOR
"Should we keep	1989	70.0	IA	Iowa
the State Lottery?"	1990	54.0	CA	CSR
	1990	58.0	KS	KP
	1993	60.0	GA	AJC/WSB
Pari-mutuels Questions				
"Should the state	1993	49.0	GA	AJC/WSB
legalize horse and dog racing?"				
"Should state allow	1993	46.6	AL	SOR
video gambling machines at dog/horse tracks?"				
"Should state make	1989	48.0	MO	MP
dog racing legal?"				
Casino Questions				
"Would you support	1993	41.1	AL	SOR
or oppose Casinos?"	1993	38.0	GA	AJC/WSB
	1989	55.0	LA	UNO
	1989	42.0	MO	MP
	1989	42.3	KS	KP
. . . in nearby city	1986	77.0	NJ	Eagle
	1990	49.0	OH	OH
	1992	32.0	IL	Trib
. . . in mountains	1990	49.0	CO	RMN
. . . in resort area	1989	44.0	WV	WVA
. . . on riverboats	1993	51.9	AL	SOR
	1989	32.0	WV	WVA

Table 5.5 (*continued*)

	Year	% Positive	State	Poll
Have they been a	1989	42.0	MO	MP
good thing. . . . ?"	1986	66.0	NJ	Eagle

Note: Some polls use the word "Favor" in place of "Support."

Sources: Statewide polls and years as shown.

they do not have any moral qualms about gambling. The poll asked respondents if they believed legalized gambling encourages some people to gamble who would not otherwise do so, a question to which 47 percent agreed strongly and another 28 percent agreed somewhat. Another question, aimed at the underlying bases of support, asked if state lotteries keep taxes down. A majority of respondents felt that lotteries do not have much effect on state taxes. All of these questions and the responses are detailed in Table 5.6.

The 1993 CNN/*USA Today* poll asked whether gambling is basically an immoral activity, a question to which only 35 percent responded yes. The poll also included questions about whether society was hurt or helped by state-sponsored gambling. Fifty-five percent responded that gambling was helpful, since legalization was a way to regulate and collect taxes from an activity people would engage in anyway.

A 1990 poll for the *Minneapolis Star-Tribune* found 59 percent of respondents felt that "gambling is just another form of entertainment, no better or no worse than going to a movie or any other entertainment that costs money" (Hugick & Saad, 1994, p. 9). A 1988 Eagleton Poll asked several questions about why people favor or oppose gambling. Some 77 percent of the respondents in New Jersey felt that the state should provide the lottery, since people want to play it, and 78 percent felt that people would gamble anyway, so there is nothing wrong with the state raising money from the lottery.

Even in non-lottery states, similar sentiments are echoed when polls ask questions about the morality and appropriateness of state-sponsored gambling. A 1989 poll by the University of Wyoming found that 54 percent of the state's residents had purchased at least one lottery ticket, yet the state did not have its own lottery. In a question about support for a proposed lottery in Wyoming that specifically asked whether it would be better to provide money for education and social programs through additional taxation or through a state lottery, 64 percent indicated the lottery was the better choice.

In Alabama, a 1993 poll by Southern Opinion Research asked several questions about legalized gambling. Only 49 percent agreed that gambling is immoral (42 percent disagreed and 9 percent did not answer), whereas 60 percent thought gambling provides needed revenue for programs such as education and senior citizens. Substantial majorities of 68 percent and 64 percent, respectively, thought gambling creates jobs and stimulates the economy and that the state might as well make money from gambling, since people are going to do it anyway.

The resounding themes in all of these surveys are that many people feel that gambling would occur with or without state sponsorship and that it can provide money for worthwhile services without increasing taxes.

This look into various national and statewide surveys regarding the basic forms of gambling reveals several things. Perhaps the most important for the purposes of this study is the notion that the public does not view all forms of gambling as being equal. Instead, the public likes some forms of gambling, such as the lottery; has mixed feelings about others, such as casinos; and is downright hostile to still other forms, such as sports betting.

The reasons that underlie support or nonsupport of gambling are likewise complex. While a demographic examination of the persons who support gambling policies suggests that a certain "type" of person is most likely to favor lotteries, casinos, and the like, these characteristics do not hold for support of all forms of gambling. Younger, higher income, educated urbanites who attend church services infrequently are most in support of lotteries. The same groups tend to support casinos and off-track betting. When researchers have asked questions attempting to discover specifically why respondents support or oppose gambling, they have generally found that gambling is viewed somewhat skeptically by the public. On the one hand, people feel that gambling would occur with or without state sponsorship and that some forms of gambling are basically harmless entertainment. On the other hand, many have serious concerns about the impacts of gambling, and few people appear to believe that gambling revenues will bring economic salvation to the states. Above all, survey researchers have found that gambling is something that many people want and is something that many more are willing to tolerate.

Table 5.6
The Bases of Support for Legal Gambling in National Polls, 1989 and 1993

Q: And do you agree strongly, agree somewhat, disagree somewhat, or disagree strongly that legalized gambling encourages some people to gamble who would not otherwise do so?

AGREE STRONGLY	47%
AGREE SOMEWHAT	28%
DISAGREE SOMEWHAT	13%
DISAGREE STRONGLY	10%
DON'T KNOW/ NA	2%

Q: Do you think that state lotteries, where they exist, help keep state taxes down, or don't they have much effect on state taxes?

HELP KEEP TAXES DOWN	29%
NOT MUCH EFFECT	51%
DEPENDS (VOLUNTEERED)	2%
DON'T KNOW/ NA	18%

Q: Do you agree or disagree with the following statement. . . . Gambling is basically immoral?

AGREE	35%
DISAGREE	62%
DON'T KNOW/ NA	3%

Q: Which comes closer to your view about the increasing number of states that are legalizing gambling, and the increasing number of lotteries and games of chance that state governments are sponsoring: Society will be hurt because gambling breeds crime, and making it more available will increase compulsive gambling in America, or Society will be helped, because gambling will occur anyway and legalizing it allows government to regulate and tax it?

HELPED	55%
HURT	37%
NEITHER/DON'T KNOW	9%

Sources: CBS News/*New York Times* poll for "48 Hours," conducted April 13–16, 1989. Sample: Nationwide random telephone sample of 1,412 adults. CNN/ *USA Today* poll by Gallop, conducted September 13–15, 1993. Sample: Nationwide random telephone sample, as reported in *The Public Perspective*, January/February 1994, p. 13.

THE GAMBLING INDUSTRY'S RESPONSE TO ECONOMIC AND SOCIAL IMPACTS

"Winners Know When to Quit" reads a Mississippi billboard. The ad, paid for by the Mississippi Council on Problem Gambling, is partially funded by the Mississippi casino industry. The American Gaming Association (AGA) in 1996 founded the National Center for Responsible Gaming (NCRG). The NCRG provides a vehicle for the casino gambling industry to fund basic and applied research into both the level and the effects of problem gambling and underage gambling. NCRG also helps to provide training for casino employees to help them recognize and deal with problem gamblers.

"We in the casino gaming industry have declared that one problem gambler is one too many," says AGA president Frank Fahrenkopf. To that end, the industry has poured some $3.7 million into 20 different university and research institute studies of problem gambling (AGA, 2001). However, as an editorial column in *The Economist* pointed out: "[E]ven on conservative measures (reached by assuming that the average casino visitor loses $200 annually), problem gamblers would account for three-eighths of casinos' revenues. How badly does the industry want to cure them?" ("Busted Flush," 1997, p. 29).

While the gaming industry acknowledges that problem gambling poses serious concerns for the industry, it forcefully denies that problem gamblers or any other facet of the gambling industry can accept the blame for the host of social ills commonly attributed to gambling. In an effort to get that message across, the AGA has funded a number of studies of the relationship between casinos and crime, casinos and bankruptcy, and similar social concerns. Much of this research is touted on the Association's website.

The AGA puts out a monthly newsletter for its members that repeatedly returns to themes involving the alleged downsides of gambling. In its June 2000 newsletter, for example, the AGA noted that an April 2000 report prepared for gaming critic Representative Frank Wolf (R–VA) by the General Accounting Office had "once again, met defeat" (AGA, 2001).

"It's become all too easy for people to point a finger at casinos as a cause for all kinds of social ills without the facts to back up their claims," Fahrenkopf told the *Christian Science Monitor*, adding that social problems purportedly related to gambling are "rarely as simple as gaming critics would like to believe" (Knickerbocker, 1999).

LEGISLATORS, ELITES, AND THEIR VIEW
OF GAMBLING

Only a small handful of national legislators have spoken publicly about the gambling industry. Most have voiced opposition to the spread and availability of gambling; most also fall within the socially conservative wing of the Republican Party. Representative John Kyl (R–AZ) has said that "gambling often has terrible consequences for families and communities . . . 5 percent of all gamblers become addicted. Many of those turn to crime and commit suicide. We all pay for those tragedies" (Knickerbocker, 1999).

Yet, it would be extraordinarily misleading to characterize the Republican Party as anti-gambling. A study published by the liberal activist group Public Citizen points an accusatory finger at Senate Minority Leader Trent Lott and the three Republican fund-raising committees with which he deals. The report argues that Lott and other Republican leaders in Congress received 65 percent of all soft money contributions from gambling interests during the two election cycles between 1995 and 1998 ("Betting on Trent Lott," 1999).

Casino industry publications frequently acknowledge Senator Lott as a behind-the-scenes supporter, but he is careful to avoid the appearance of outright support. For example, Lott's Senate Web page and constituent mailings do not even reference his home state's huge gambling industry. Public Citizen says of Lott that he has "pursued his pro-casino interests discreetly . . . avoided public debates, votes, and press inquiries" on the subject ("Betting on Trent Lott," 1999).

Democrats, overall, are no more eager to publicly stump for gambling than their Republican counterparts. In 1998, then-House Minority Leader Richard Gephardt (D–MO) and other top House Democrats toured the mega-casino resort Mirage before joining donors at a gourmet buffet. Gephardt, and the ranking Democrat on the House Ways and Means Committee, Charles Rangel of New York, returned in 1999 to meet with then-chairman of Mirage Resorts Steve Wynn to accept his $250,000 contribution for House Democrats ("Paying the Price," 2000). When Gephardt used this opportunity to name a member of the National Gambling Impact Study Commission, he chose gaming employee union president John Wilhelm because "it's important for the workers to have a voice in this process" (Lambrecht & Poor, 1997). Gephardt said that he was not trying to appoint an industry-friendly commission member.

Former Senator Paul Simon (D–IL) has been a vocal critic of gambling. In a 1995 speech on the Senate floor, Simon said that gambling can be addictive and that such compulsive gambling leads to increases in crime and suicide (Simon, 1995).

Democrats in state governments are no more, or less, likely to publicly voice support than their federal counterparts. While Democratic governors have won several well-publicized battles to create new lotteries in states such as Georgia (Zell Miller) and South Carolina (Jim Hodges), Governor Parris Glendening (D–MD) has forcefully opposed expansion of gambling in his state.

THE POLITICS OF GAMBLING'S SOCIAL IMPACTS

The public generally supports gambling while expressing some reservations about certain forms of it; the industry claims that any harm from gambling is grossly exaggerated; and politicians from both parties accept gambling industry contributions while avoiding the appearance of being too supportive of the industry, even while other members from both parties decry legalized gambling's myriad social ill effects. Why do state lotteries and legal casinos continue to create such ambivalent reactions? Part of the answer may be seen in the equally ambivalent findings of research into gambling's effects.

Invariably, gambling's economic impacts and the bureaucratic and political support system that is built around the industry join forces to shield casinos, card rooms, and other gambling forms from any potential public backlash. Meier (1988) has asserted that capture is unlikely to occur in social regulatory policy arenas, such as insurance policy, because these policies result from "a complex interaction of industry groups, consumer interests, regulatory bureaucrats, and political elites" (p. 167). Central to his assertion, however, was both an industry lacking a unified set of policy goals and a public with a strong desire to keep insurance prices low. Both of these constraints on the possibility of capture are lacking in the case of the gambling industry. Unlike many other social regulatory policies, gambling is a policy that is set at the state level, and gambling policy regulation is set by agencies whose daily activities do not command a great deal of public or media attention.

A recent theory asserts that the amount of political control over bureaucracies will vary according to the salience and complexity of the issues under the control of a particular bureaucracy. Where public salience is high and complexity is low (as in the case of gambling), elected officials can and will exercise control over bureaucratic decision making and attempt to limit discretionary authority (Eisner, Worsham, & Ringquist, 1999, p. 30). Yet, both the case studies and the review of industry regulation provided earlier suggest that once gambling has been authorized, there is little propensity for elected officials to frequently intercede in gambling regulation.

Nevertheless, gambling regulation is not viewed in quite the same way as insurance or telecommunications. For a sizable minority of the population, gambling is a question of right and wrong. For others it is a business they want access to but also want to ensure is run fairly. For still others, it is a business that should be legal but strictly limited because its potential harmful side effects must be minimized.

These three views are expressed well in both the public opinion data and in the public statements and private actions of political elites. The public, and the various groups within the larger public, do respond to gambling in a way that is not typically true of economic policies. The gambling adoption model presented in Chapter 3 demonstrates that some "traditional" factors—such as state income, fiscal need, and diffusion pressures—are at work in the spread of gambling, and, yet, these factors alone cannot account for either the states that have chosen gambling or those that have not.

It now seems clear that in order for gambling to have substantial economic impacts it must be operated openly and competitively, it must transform itself into "entertainment" and "tourism," and it must draw substantial numbers of new visitors to the state. In order for states to allow such unrestricted gambling, significant political hurdles must be overcome. Sometimes, as in the case of Nevada, a socially liberal state populace and a dismal general state economy combine to provide the opportunity.

This study suggests that gambling can be a significant source of economic development if, and only if, it manages to attract visitors and/or to entice players to spend money gambling that they otherwise would not have spent. If that happens, then morality will likely become overshadowed by economic policy concerns. Economics, of course, is not completely static. Individual consumers have options—spending versus saving, for example—and the manner in which they choose to exercise their options will shape the outcome of any gambling policy. The way the policy is created and implemented will also shape the way consumers exercise their options. Thus, the present study also suggests that gambling will have the greatest economic impact, and possibly the lowest level of negative social impacts for local residents, when it is encouraged to grow via competitive regulatory structure.

These findings create hard realities for policy makers. Authorizing a new form of gambling is not as simple as asking "shall we, or shall we not?" because the type, level, and limits on the proposed form of gambling will dramatically alter its impacts, and it is those impacts that have enormous political consequences for all involved.

NOTES

1. This figure includes about 400,500 employees of commercial and tribal casinos. The majority work in Nevada, New Jersey, or Mississippi; the remainder is employed by other gambling establishments, including state lotteries and pari-mutuel facilities.

2. While this seems an extraordinarily high amount from such a small group, it is noteworthy that these were self-reported figures from the state prevalence study. It is likely that both problem and nonproblem gamblers as a group were misreporting their expenditures, and perhaps only a small portion (the heavy spenders) in this study accurately portrayed their losses.

3. The methodology carefully accounts for actual costs (such as the cost of prosecuting gamblers who embezzle or write bad checks to pay for their gambling) and uses conservative estimates where appropriate (such as including only one-half of the debts problem gamblers declared when they filed for bnkruptcy).

4. Wisconsin has 17 Indian tribal casinos. These estimates are based on patrons at those facilities.

5. Two other studies by the same authors examined, first, Wisconsin casinos' impacts on a variety of social problems and the relation between casinos and pathological gambling, and, second, the relationship between the casinos and crime. Those studies are examined in more detail in Chapter 6.

6. Interested readers are referred especially to "Pathological Gambling: A Critical Review," a report of the National Academy of Sciences (1999).

7. See Smith (2001, pp. 191–192) for his development of a similar line of reasoning with regard to the regulation of pornography.

8. The question asked was: "Do you agree or disagree with the following statement. . . . 'Gambling is basically immoral?' "

6

Rolling the Dice: Assessments and Directions for the Future of Legal Gambling

At the close of the Great Depression, legal gambling was available in only eight states; seven states allowed pari-mutuel wagering on horse races; and Nevada had authorized casinos. At the start of the twenty-first century, all U.S. states except Hawaii, Tennessee, and Utah allow some form of legal gambling. When Indian casinos are factored in, a dozen states allow three or more forms of gambling. State governments, eager to find new funding sources, have been primarily responsible for the expanded availability of gambling in the United States.

In 1972, Gilbert Geis published a monograph for the Center for Studies of Crime and Delinquency in which he argued for the decriminalization of most forms of gambling. "There are dangers to the individual from legalized gambling," he wrote, "but they are no more intense than those attendant upon criminalized gambling. And, even if they were so, . . . individuals ought to be allowed to go their way unmolested to the extent that they do not directly harm others or do not place the polity in clearly recognizable and immediate jeopardy" (p. 250).

Today, the key political question involves not whether gambling should or should not be legal because clearly the legalization of most forms of gambling has been both rapid and widespread; rather, the pertinent question today is, To what extent should government be the promoter and promulgator of gambling, rather than simply allowing but regulating the activity? The dilemma is somewhat reminiscent of the "chicken and the egg" question; does government expand and promote gambling because public acceptance has increased, or has acceptance grown as a result of a legitimization process spurred by government revenue imperatives?

In the executive summary to its final report, the National Gambling Impact Study Commission (NGISC) stated that the "line between the state as regulator and the state as gambling franchise has grown increasingly nebulous," and expressed concern that there was an inherent conflict "between the desire to maximize revenue and the need to promote the public good" (NGISC, 1999, p. 15).

In various national and statewide surveys, the percentage of respondents who say that they believe gambling is immoral ranges from a low of 9 percent to a high of only 20 percent (von Herrmann, 1997). This evidence begs the question as to whether gambling policy has moved into the realm of "consensus" morality policy, or whether it is more a "redistributive" morality policy. It shows the public is less judgmental about gambling and more receptive to potential claims of economic benefit.

Economist Adam Rose has asked, "[I]s a casino more like a factory, or a restaurant?" (NGISC, 1999, p. 6). In purely economic terms, he discovered, the answer is that it depends. If developed in a competitive market, a casino can attract tourism and can "import" money and jobs into an economy. If, however, casinos are restricted either by regulatory structure or by location, they tend to simply recycle existing sources of funds in the economy and thus create relatively few new dollars or jobs.

For students of public policy, a relevant question is, Is a casino more like a liquor store or an investment firm? In other words, it is helpful to understand whether gambling is a human vice—a weakness—that needs to be limited and controlled by government in order to protect persons from their own bad tendencies, or whether it is simply a market that involves certain inherent risks, and that must therefore be regulated in order to minimize those risks to the public. The former is an issue of first principles, the latter is not. In attempting to answer that question, this study has considered the participants, their expectations and beliefs, their level of interaction, the resources they bring, the strategies they employ, and the benefits they expect to receive.

Gambling is not new in the United States or elsewhere, but it is experiencing renewed interest and vigor. The gambling industry as a whole is both financially sound and politically savvy. Using its own team of lobbyists and public relations firms, the industry has attempted to transform itself from gambling into gaming—from "sin" into "amusement"—and has been largely successful. Politicians, too, have been instrumental in moving gambling away from the locus of public and private morals and toward a focus on economic and regulatory concerns. One after another, state governments have promoted gambling, either outright (as in the case of state lotteries) or surreptitiously via tourism or economic development plans.

Regulatory and tax structures tend to focus on keeping gambling clean and free of entanglements with organized crime, while promoting maximum revenue generation. Few in state or federal government have publicly considered the moral questions underlying the new government reliance on gambling revenues.

Public acceptance of gambling is at an all-time high, and open public discourse about the underlying values involved is rather low. The findings of the National Gambling Impact Study Commission beautifully illustrate that, on balance, they were cautious, predictable, and pragmatic. In general, the study scrupulously avoids questions of morals and values. Yet, much of what has been said publicly elsewhere about gambling involves precisely that: questions of morals and values.

The gambling issue has become bifurcated, but not in the way that is more typically seen in other areas of morality policy; instead gambling policy "debates" today tend to involve two distinct groups talking to each other about distinctly separate issues. Political and economic elites talk about job creation, voluntary taxation, and providing a "clean" outlet for our natural inclinations to gambling. Philosophical conservatives and Fundamentalist religious members talk about devaluing the work ethic and devastating families through the social ills they associate with gambling.

In some respect, attitudes about gambling appear to track those regarding a host of morality issues. Abortion, homosexual rights, drug policy, pornography, and euthanasia, for example, have all experienced similar effects as the American polity has undergone a postmodern transformation. Debates over first principles have increasingly been overwhelmed by debates over timing and implementation. Gay rights laws, for instance, are to some extent now viewed by most people as an issue of civil rights and individual choice. Opinion in the area of gay rights is approaching consensus, but for some groups the subject is still viewed in purely moral terms. The same is largely true for gambling.

As the 1999 lottery defeat in Alabama illustrates, mobilizing public opinion against proposed changes in morality policy now often requires discussion of policy details, rather than underlying values. Most actions to legalize gambling are not given long and thoughtful consideration, if the case studies presented in this book are typical. Rather, as in Mississippi, gambling is often introduced, or expanded, in a quick and quiet manner that minimizes the opportunity for public discourse.

In Nevada, the 2001 legislative session was marked by what has become a perennial issue: whether to raise the tax on Nevada gross gaming revenues. State Senator Joe Neal (a Democrat from the North Las Vegas district) wants the rate increased from 6.25 percent to 11.25 percent. A June 2000 poll for the *Las Vegas Review Journal* showed that 63 percent of Nevada residents supported the tax increase, whereas only 26 percent opposed it. Even in "Sin City" the policy debate is all about economics. "We have to be careful," Neal said in an interview, ". . . [the casinos] are beginning to feed on our population. . . . You have got to control gaming, or gaming will control you" (Simpson, 2001, p. 3).

Perhaps the surest sign of Senator Neal's assertion comes in the various efforts of Steve Wynn, the former head of Mirage Resorts, and of the $1.9 billion mega-resort Bellagio in Las Vegas, as well as the $650 million Beau Rivage resort in Mississippi. Wynn's Mirage not only made the largest single campaign contribution in the 1997 mayoral race for Beau Rivage's future "hometown" of Biloxi, Mississippi, but it also successfully lobbied the Mississippi state legislature to enact laws allowing microbreweries, the first of which is located inside Beau Rivage (Pulley, 1998b).

A study done in Oregon found that one result common to every one of the state's financial crises over the past couple of decades was that a new form of gambling had been legalized, and, consequently, Oregon currently has more forms of legal gambling than any other state outside of Nevada (see Lotteries, 1999). Clearly, gambling presents conflicting goals that can only be reconciled by political officials in a republic such as ours. There have been surprisingly few attempts to grapple with this problem.

The evidence presented in Chapters 1 through 5 makes a strong case for the morality policy process model. In terms of public participation in gambling policy adoptions and formulation, several factors have served to limited public involvement. First, gambling is typically framed as a question of economic need and potential economic benefit. The halo of good causes—in which gambling policy is tied to some worthy public policy goal—enhances the ability of elites to obscure the complex nature of many gambling policies.

Gambling policy can be seen as responsive to mass public opinion, when one defines responsiveness in terms of policy adoption in which a majority expresses support. As the public's view of gambling has softened, the prevalence and availability of gambling have increased. Gambling policies are responsive to negative public opinion as well: Numerous state and local votes against lotteries, casinos, and convenience gambling provide stark evidence that politicians are generally unwilling to enact gambling policies in the absence of demonstrated local majority support, or where strong groups such as pro-family or church groups can mobilize strong opposition.

The expectations and beliefs of the participants in gambling policy are continually shaped by both the history and the evolution of gambling. Gambling continues to experience the consequences of its nineteenth- and early-twentieth-century history of corruption and scandal. Gambling industry leaders sometimes grumble about the heavy regulation imposed on their business. Frank Fahrenkopf of the American Gaming Association has repeatedly said: "Gaming–entertainment is one of the most tightly-regulated industries in the United States" (American Gaming Association, 2000). States have been increasingly willing, though, to remove restrictions when they are shown to unnecessarily limit revenues without providing substantial protection against social consequences (as in the removal by several states of the restrictions on riverboat gambling loss limits or cruise requirements).

In general, interaction between the public and various policy makers has been somewhat limited in the area of gambling policy reformulation. Gambling policies have developed incrementally; once made legal, most forms of gambling have been quietly expanded, and regulations that could limit revenue growth have been loosened.

Gambling policy debates make strange bedfellows. One of the more profitable and long-standing of the Alabama state racetracks was located in Greene County. During the 1999 legislative session, the track's owner sought legislative approval to add video-gambling terminals at the tracks, but the measure was defeated, largely on the strength of opposition presented by a coalition of conservative religious groups.

Later that year, the Greene County commissioners sued a number of anti-gambling groups—along with several Southern Baptist preachers and members of legal casino operations in neighboring Mississippi—claiming a conspiracy to defraud the public and avert gambling revenues from Greene racetracks into Mississippi casinos (Walton, 2000). In October 1999, the Alabama State Supreme Court threw out the case. The mere filing of this lawsuit presents a clear example of how emotionally charged the gambling issue can become and how unexpected the gambling coalitions can sometimes be (who could imagine the elected county commission in any southern state suing a list of local Baptist preachers?).

The gambling industry has become a political constituency to be served, and a force to be reckoned with, at the start of the twenty-first century. As outlined briefly in Chapter 2, gambling lobbyists, political action committees and corporations have cumulatively spent billions of dollars on various candidates for federal, state, and local offices, and to support state or local referenda to authorize gaming. The gambling industry provides support to, and has found supporters within the ranks of, both political parties. The industry has also become the primary funding source for research into problem and pathological gambling, and a major funding source for other social and economic impact research.

Gambling proponents have successfully used not only the economic incentive for continued expansion but also the lack of credible research that could refute industry claims about the benefits of gambling. Likewise, the industry has made a strong case that the poor quality and inconsistent methodologies used by much of the social impact research invalidates the claims of opponents. For their part, most gambling opponents are willing to use arguments about negative social impacts or regarding potential corruption or insufficient oversight, but in the end most see their opposition to gambling as a moral stand.

Neither framework alone has been particularly helpful for policy making. Industry claims must be viewed with healthy skepticism, since they tend to be self-serving. Opponents' assertions also deserve critical skepticism, since they tend to be based on feelings about what is right and what is wrong, rather than on hard evidence. Policy making, at least theoretically, should be about determination of the public good.

A morality policy process framework can provide a mechanism for the careful study of both underlying values and the processes that allow them expression. This research effort is by no means the definitive work on the morality policy process involved in gambling adoption and regulation. A major weakness of this effort has been its inability to adequately capture, beyond case studies and other anecdotal evidence, the specific agenda setting (Glick & Hutchinson, 2001) and reframing (Meier, 1994) techniques that have been used to reclassify gambling policy from a consensus morality issue to a redistributive policy (Doan & Meier, 1998). Likewise, much more work is needed to understand how the implementation of gambling policy affects its continuing evolution (Smith, 2001). These and many other areas of gambling policy are ripe for further research.

William Eadington, who directs the Institute for the Study of Gambling and Commercial Gaming at the University of Nevada–Reno, has said that legal casinos "became more corporate from the 1970s onward," and because of this casinos "were less able to ignore the growing anecdotal and scientific evidence that linked an increase in permitted gambling with apparent increases in the incidence of problem gambling" (Eadington, 2000, p. 15). Eadington also maintains that a desire to address problem gambling and its consequences has largely driven policy along two lines: wholesale constraints on the ability to gamble, such as betting limits or locale restrictions, and various attempts to target and limit the actual problem gambler, including industry training and self-banning proposals. Neither has been shown to successfully limit the impacts or the level of problem gamblers.

H. George Frederickson has said that while the world is "too complex to attempt to reconstruct the Greek city-state, . . . it is possible to rebuild the public through an understanding of human interdependence" and, ultimately, he adds, "interdependence may drive us into each other's arms" (Frederickson, 1997, p. 51). Likewise, those who would make public policy cannot work from the perspective that all citizens are individually responsible for all of their actions, since our world, which is both expanding and shrinking at the same time, provides few, if any, real opportunities for that brand of rugged individualism.

To say that the state government, which created, expanded, and heavily promoted the lottery or casino, is somehow not responsible for the harsh effects of that lottery or casino on a relatively small number of problem gamblers, is to abdicate the very essence of our form of government—that is, the protection of minorities from the potential excesses of majorities. Likewise to say that government should wholly ban access to gambling, when the vast majority of adults seem not only to enjoy it but to suffer no obvious ill effects from their gambling activity, is clearly an overreach that moves beyond what most Americans want or expect their government to be.

The proper role for gambling policy lies somewhere in between these two extremes. Clearly, it should be informed by the risks inherent both in a prohibition of gambling (Would illegal gambling flourish? Would we see a large new class of "criminals" with whose incarcerations and paroles we would now have to deal?) and in unfettered and unregulated gambling (Would rigged games become more commonplace? Would unseemly operators dramatically overextend credit to problem gamblers?).

Students of gambling policy must not forget that public policies exist only in human terms. People are more than mere consumers, and they are more than victims. They are beings capable of thought—of reason and discernment—and, thus, our analysis must be informed by our moral position. Are the two objectives contradictory? They need not be, if we are willing to engage in open debate about the proper role of government and about the relative merits of both individual liberties and collective responsibilities.

The freedom of any individual adult to engage in legal gambling must be weighed carefully alongside the responsibility of maintaining an orderly and productive society. As long as gambling is pursued as recreation, society should have no compelling interest to prohibit it. But when gambling becomes problematic—when the number of persons who experience problem or pathological gambling becomes large, for example, or when the presence of a very large gambling industry begins to cause serious damage to local quality of life—then society can, and should, weigh the relative costs and benefits of continuing to allow the expansion of gambling.

Bibliography

Abt, V., Smith, J.F., & Christiansen, E.M. (1985). *The Business of Risk: Commercial Gambling in Mainstream America*. Lawrence: University of Kansas Press.

Alabama Rejects Governor's Plan for a Lottery. (1999, October 9). CNN Online News. Accessed January 26, 2000. Available: http://www.cnn/allpolitics.com/.

American Gaming Association. (1996). Press releases [Online]. Available: http://www.americangaming.org/.

American Gaming Association. Update. (1999, December 13) [Online]. Available: http://www.americangaming.org/.

American Gaming Association. (2000, February) Press release [Online]. Available: http://www/americangaming.org/media_updatenews_release/news_index.cfm.

American Gaming Association. (2001). Press releases [Online]. Available: http://www.americangaming.org/.

AP News Online. (1998, November 10). Siegelman & Lottery Win Big [Online]. Available: http://www.nytimes.com/pages/aponline/news/.

Anderson, Arthur. (1996). *Economic Impacts of Casino Gaming in the United States. Volume. 1: Macro Study. Report to the American Gaming Association*. Washington, D.C.: Author.

Anderson, Arthur. (1997). *Economic Impacts of Casino Gaming in the United States—Volume 2: Micro Study. Report to the American Gaming Association*. Washington, D.C.: Author.

Baker, J.N. (1990, February 5). Gambling on Riverboats: War between the States. *Newsweek*, 115: 22.

Batt, T. (1999, June 16). Gambling Foe Seeks Federal Tax. *Las Vegas Review Journal*. [Online]. Available: http://www.lvrj.com/lvrj_home/1999/Jun-16-Wed-1999/news/11381973.html.

Berenseon, A. (1996, April 16). Colorado Casinos Beat the Odds—State Gamblers Double U.S. Average. *Denver Post*. [Online]. Available: http://www.newslibrary.com/.

Berry, F.S., & Berry, W.D. (1990). State Lottery Adoptions as Policy Innovations: An Event History Analysis. *American Political Science Review*, 84(2): 395–416.

Betting on Trent Lott: The Casino Gambling Industry's Campaign Contributions Pay off in Congress. (1999). *Public Citizen*. [Online]. Available: http://www.citizen.org/congress/campaign/special_interest/articles.cfm?ID 544.

Black, C.L., Jr. (1974). *Capital Punishment: The Inevitability of Caprice and Mistake*. New York: Norton.

Blevins, A., & Jensen, K. (1998, March). Gambling as a Community Development Quick Fix. *Annals of the American Academy of Political and Social Science*, 556: 109–123.

Boehmke, F.J. (1999, March 6). *The Initiative as a Catalyst for Policy Change*. Paper presented at the annual meeting of the Western Political Science Association, Seattle, WA.

Bolton, A. (1993, October 12). Alabama Gamblers Come to State for Lottery Tickets. *Atlanta Journal and Constitution*, p. 2-A.

Borg, M.O., Mason, P.M., & Shapiro, S.L. (1991). The Incidence of Taxes on Casino Gambling: Exploiting the Tired and the Poor. *American Journal of Economics and Sociology*, 50: 323–333.

Boswell, B. (1996, August 22). Hope for Alabama: Legislator to Propose New Scholarship. *Crimson White*, p. 1.

Boushy, J. (1993). Harrah's Survey of U.S. Casino Gaming Entertainment Reveals Gamblers Like the Interactive Nature of Casino Gaming. *International Gaming and Wagering Business*, 14: 8–13.

Bowers, W.J. (1984). *Legal Homicide: Death as Punishment in America, 1864–1982*. Boston: Northeastern University Press.

Branson, R. (1999, January 22). Mississippi Forces New Casinos to Make Big Land Investment. *Memphis (Tennessee) Commercial Appeal*, p. 4.

Brenner, R., & Brenner, G. (1990). *Gambling and Speculation*. New York: Cambridge University Press.

Brisbin, R.A., Jr. (2001). From Censorship to Ratings: Substantive Rationality, Political Entrepreneurship, and Sex in the Movies. In C. Mooney (Ed.), *The Public Clash of Private Values* (pp. 91–114). New York: Chatham House.

Broomhall, D. (1996). *Is Riverboat Gambling an Effective Economic Development Strategy for Indiana Communities?* West Lafayette, IN: Purdue University.

Bryant, P. (1998). *A Limited Performance Review of the Gaming Industry's Economic Impact.* Jackson, MS: Office of the State Auditor of Mississippi.

Busted Flush. (1997, January 25). *The Economist.* 26–28.

Butler, D., & Ranney, A. (1994). *Referendums around the World.* Washington, DC: AEI Press.

Bybee, S.L., & Mayer, K. (1998). *Gaming's Impact upon a Local Economy: Greenville, Mississippi.* Las Vegas: University of Nevada International Gaming Institute.

Bybee, S. L., & Agureo, J. (1998). *The Hospitality Industry's Impact on the State of Nevada.* Las Vegas: University of Nevada International Gaming Institute.

Calonius, E. (1991). The Big Payoff from Lotteries. *Fortune,* 123: 112.

Carmines, E.G., & Stimson, J.A. (1980). The Two Faces of Issue Voting. *American Political Science Review,* 74(1): 78–91.

Casino Control Commission (New Jersey). (1999). Available at http://www.state.nj.us/casinos/.

Casino to Be Built at Rivergate. (1993, February 12). *Times-Picayune (Louisiana),* p. 1.

Caudill, S.B., Ford, J. M., Mixon, Fr. G., & Peng, T.C. (1995). A Discrete-time Hazard Model of Lottery Adoption. *Applied Economics,* 27: 555–561.

Christiansen, E.M. (1998). Gambling and the American Economy. *Annals of the American Academy of Politial and Social Science,* 556: 36–52.

Christiansen, E.M. (1999). *Gambling and Gaming in the United States.* Various years consulted; reprints provided by E.M. Christiansen, Christiansen Capital Advisers.

Clotfelter, C.T., & Cook, P.E. (1989). *Selling Hope: The Lottery in America.* Cambridge, MA: Harvard University Press.

Clotfelter, C.T., Cook, P.E., Edell, J.A., & Moore, M. (1999). *State Lotteries at the Turn of the Century. Report to the National Gambling Impact Study Commission.* Washington, D.C.: National Gambling Impact Study Commission.

Clynch, E.J., & Rivenbark, W.C. (1999). Need Money? Roll the Dice. *International Journal of Public Administration,* 22: 1681–1703.

Cobb, M.D., & Kuklinski, J.H. (1997). Changing Minds: Political Arguments and Political Persuasion. *American Journal of Political Science,* 41(1): 88–122.

Colorado Gaming Commission. (2001). Overview [Online]. Available: http://www.gaming.state.co.us.

Colorado Lottery Commission. (2001). The History of the Colorado Lottery [Online]. Available: http://www.coloradolottery.com.

Commission on the Review of National Policy toward Gambling. (1976). *Gambling in America*. Washington, DC: Author.

Common Cause. (1997). Gamblers Unanimous: Gambling Interests Tripled Their Soft-Money Giving in 1996 [Online]. Available: http://www.commoncause.org/publications/

Connor, M. (1993). Bright Days for California Card Clubs. *International Gaming and Wagering Business*, 14: 48–51.

Cook, J. (1992). Legalizing the Slots. *Forbes*, 149: 78–82.

Cotter, P.R., & Stovall, J.G. (1998, November 8). Siegelman Brilliantly Blended Lottery and Education. *Montgomery (Alabama) Advertiser*.

"Could It Have Been Different?" (1999, October 14). *Mobile (Alabama) Press-Register*, p. A1.

Cowley, P. (2001). Morality Policy without Politics? The Case of Britain. In C. Mooney (Ed.), *The Public Clash of Private Values* (pp. 213–226). New York: Chatham House.

Cowley, P., & Stuart, M. (1997). Sodomy, Slaughter, Sunday Shopping, and Seatbelts: Free Votes in the House of Commons, 1979 to 1996. *Party Politics*, 3(1): 119–130.

Crist, S. (1989, May 29). Race Tracks Step Lively to Keep Up With Bettors. *New York Times*, p. 11.

Dahl, R.A. (1965). *Pluralist Democracy in America*. Chicago: Rand McNally.

DeBoer, L. (1985). Administrative Costs of State Lotteries. *National Tax Journal*, 38: 489–497.

Demaris, O. (1986). *The Boardwalk Jungle*. New York: Bantam Books.

Dense, J. (1997). State Lotteries and Public Policy: An Academic Appraisal. In W.R. Eadington & J. Cornelius (Eds.), *Gambling Public Policies and the Social Sciences* (pp. 575–606). Reno, NV: The Institute for the Study of Gambling and Commercial Gaming.

Doan, A.E., & Meier, K.J. (1998, April). Violence as a Political Strategy: The Case of Anti-Abortion Activists. Paper presented at the annual meeting of the Midwest Political Science Association, Chicago, IL.

Dombrink, J., & Thompson, W.N. (1990). *The Last Resort: Success and Failure in Campaigns for Casinos*. Reno: University of Nevada Press.

Driskell, L., & Ivey, D. (1995). Analysis of Gaming Industry Development: A Mississippi Case Study. *Economic Development Review*, 34: 40–45.

Dunstan, R. (1997). *Gambling in California: An Overview*. Sacramento: California Research Bureau.

Dye, T.R. (1966). *Politics, Economics, and the Public: Policy Outcomes in the American States*. Chicago: Rand McNally.

Eadington, W.R. (1995). Economic Development and the Introduction of

Casinos: Myths and Realities. *Economic Development Review*, 34: 3–8.

Eadington, W.R. (1998, March). Contributions of Casino-Style Gambling to Local Economies. *Annals of the American Academy of Political and Social Science*, 556: 53–65.

Eadington, W.R. (1999). The Economics of Casino Gambling. *Journal of Economic Perspectives*, 13: 173–192.

Eadington, W.R. (2000, August 15). Measuring Costs from Permitted Gaming: Concepts and Categories in Evaluating Gambling's Consequences. Paper prepared for the Canadian Centre on Substance Abuse, Ottowa, Ontario.

Edelman, M. (1964). *The Symbolic Uses of Politics*. Urbana: University of Illinois Press.

Eisner, M. A. (1993). *Regulatory Politics in Transition*. Baltimore: Johns Hopkins University Press.

Eisner, M.A., Worsham, J., & Ringquist, E.J. (1999). *Contemporary Regulatory Policy*. Boulder, Colorado: Lynne Reinner Press.

Epstein, L., & Kobylka, J.F. (1992). *Supreme Court and Legal Change: Abortion and the Death Penalty*. Chapel Hill: University of North Carolina Press.

Ezell, J.S. (1960). *Fortune's Merry Wheel: The Lottery in America*. Cambridge, MA: Harvard University Press.

Fairbanks, J.D. (1977). Religious Forces and Morality Policies in the American States. *Western Political Quarterly*, 30(2): 411–417.

Farrell, R.A., & Case, C. (1995). *The Black Book and the Mob: The Untold Story of the Control of Nevada's Casinos*. Madison: University of Wisconsin Press.

Filer, J.E., Moak, D.L. & Uze, B. (1988). Why Some States Adopt Lotteries and Others Don't. *Public Finance Quarterly*, 16: 259–284.

$570 Million Impact Seen from Gambling. (1998, March 19). *(Iowa) Gazette* [Online]. Available: http://www/newslibrary.com/.

Florida Office of Planning and Budgeting. (1992). *Casinos in Florida: An Analysis of the Economic and Social Impacts*. Tallahassee, FL: Executive Office of the Governor.

Foster, D. (1991, January 14). Passage of Law Allowing Gambling Triggers Real Estate Buying Frenzy in This Moribund Tourist Town—The Boom Is Back in Cripple Creek. *Denver Rocky Mountain News* [Online]. Available: http://archives.rockymountainnews.com.

Foster, D. (2000, November 12). Glitz vs. History: Colorado Casino Windfall Imperils 3 Towns' Frontier Legacy That Gambling Was Supposed to Save. *Denver Rocky Mountain News*, p. 3.

Franckiewicz, V.J., Jr. (1993). The States Ante Up: An Analysis of Casino Gaming Statutes. *Loyola Law Review*, 38: 1123–1157.

Frederickson, H.G. (1997). *The Spirit of Public Administration*. San Francisco: Jossey-Bass.

Frey, J.H., & Eadington, W.R. (1984). Gambling: Views from the Social Sciences. *Annals of the American Academy of Political and Social Sciences*, 556: 1–12.

Frustration Builds Over Chicago-Area Casino Proposal. (2000, July 10). *Las Vegas Review-Journal* [Online]. Available: http://www.lvrj.com.

Furlong, E.J. (1997). A Logistic Regression Model Explaining Recent State Casino Gaming Adoptions. *Policy Studies Journal*, 25: 371–383.

Gamblers Unanimous: Gambling Interests Tripled Their Soft Money Giving in 1996. (1997, June 26). *Common Cause*: Press Release.

Gambling in America. (1976). Final Report, Commission on the Review of the National Policy Toward Gambling. Washington, DC.

Gambling in the South, II. (1993, October 5). *Atlanta Journal and Constitution*, p. 2-A.

Gambling Under Attack. (1996, September 6). *Congressional Quarterly Researcher*, 6 (33): 769–792.

Gaming Faces Challenges, Opportunities in South & Midwest. (1998, May 4). *Casino Journal's National Gaming Summary*, p. 1.

Gaming Opponents Strike Out Third Time in Mississippi. (1999, May 17). *Casino Journal* [Online]. Available: http://www.casinojournal.com0/.

Garner, J. (1989, November 5). Gambling Studied for Central City. *Denver Rocky Mountain News* [Online]. Available: http://archives.rocky mountainnews.com.

Garner, J. (2001, January 17). Colorado Casino Windfall Imperils 3 Towns' Frontier Legacy. *Casino Magazine* [Online]. Available: http://www. casinomagazine.com.

Gazel, R. (1998). The Economic Impacts of Casinos Gambling at the State and Local Levels. *Annals of the American Academy of Political and Social Science*, 556: 66–79.

Geis, G. (1972). *Not the Law's Business? An Examination of Homosexuality, Abortion, Prostitution, Narcotics, and Gambling in the United States*. Rockville, MD: Center for Studies of Crime and Delinquency.

General Accounting Office. (2000, April 23). Impact of Gambling: Economic Effects More Measureable Than Social Effects. Report to the Honorable Frank R. Wolf. [Online]. Available: http://www.access. gpo.gov.

Githens, M., & Stetson, D.M. (Eds.). (1996). *Abortion Politics: Public Policy in Cross-Country Perspective*. London: Routledge.

Glass, M.E. (1981). *Nevada's Turbulent '50s*. Reno: University of Nevada Press.

Glick, H.R., & Hays, S.P. (1991). Innovation and Reinvention in State Policymaking: Theory and Evolution of Living Will Laws. *Journal of Politics*, 53: 835–850.

Glick, H.R., & Hutchinson, A. (1999). The Rising Agenda of Physician-Assisted Suicide: Explaining the Growth and Content of Morality Policy. *Policy Studies Journal*, 27(4): 750–765.

Glick, H.R., & Hutchinson, A. (2001). Physician Assisted Suicide: Agenda Setting and the Elements of Morality Policy. In C. Mooney (Ed.), *The Public Clash of Private Values* (pp. 55–7). New York: Chatham House.

Gold, S.D. (1988). It's Not a Miracle, It's a Mirage. *State Legislatures*, 14: 15.

Goodman, R. (1995). *The Luck Business: The Devastating Consequences and Broken Promises of America's Gambling Explosion*. New York: Free Press.

Gormley, W.T. (1986). Regulatory Issue Networks in a Federal System. *Polity*, 18: 595–620.

Grimm, A. (1984, October 29). Legalized Gambling Gradually Emerging in the South. *Miami Herald*, p. 1.

Grinols, E., & Omorov, J. (1996). Development or Dreamfield Delusions? Assessing Casino's Gambling Costs and Benefits. *Journal of Law and Commerce*, 16: 49–87.

Gusfield, J.R. (1963). *Symbolic Crusade: Status Politics and the American Temperance Movement*. Urbana: University of Illinois Press.

Haider-Markel, D.P. (1999). Morality Policy and Individual-Level Political Behavior: The Case of Legislative Voting on Lesbian and Gay Issues. *Policy Studies Journal*, 27(4): 735–749.

Haider-Markel, D.P., & Doan, A.M. (1998, April). *Bonfire of the Righteous: Geographically Expanding the Scope of the Conflict over Same-Sex Marriage*. Paper presented at the annual meeting of the Midwest Political Science Association, Chicago, IL.

Haider-Markel, D. P., & Meier, K. J. (1996). The Politics of Gay and Lesbian Rights: Expanding the Scope of Conflict. *Journal of Politics*, 58(2): 332–349.

Harrah's, Inc. (1999). *Harrah's Survey of Casino Entertainment*. Las Vegas, NV: Author.

Harrah's: Goodbye Colorado. (1997, January 31). *Denver Business Journal* [Online]. Available: http://ehostvgw14epn . . . /fulltext.asp.

Hill, K.Q., Leighley, J.E., & Hinton-Andersson, A. (1995). Lower-Class Mobilization and Policy Linkage in the U.S. States. *American Journal of Political Science*, 39(1): 75–86.

Hofferbert, R.I. (1966). The Relation between Public Policy and Some Structural and Environmental Variables in the American States. *American Political Science Review*, 60: 73–82.

Hopper, S. (1990, April 13). Gambling Would Stimulate Economy. *Weekly Register—Call*, p. 2

Hugick, L., & Saad, L. (1994). America's Gambling Boom. *The Public Perspective*, 5: 6–13.

Huntington, S.P. (1952, April). The Marasmus of the ICC. *Yale Law Journal*, 61: 467–509.

Hwang, S.D., & Gray, V. (1991). External Limits and Internal Determinants of State Public Policy. *Western Political Quarterly*, 44(2): 277–299.

Illinois Gaming Board. (1996). *The Economic & Fiscal Impacts of Riverboat Casino Gambling in Illinois.* Springfield, IL: Gaming Board.

Illinois Gaming Board Reaffirms Plans to Regulate Industry. (2000, January 24). *Casino Magazine* [Online]. Available: http://www.casino magazine.com.

Johnson, C.M., & Meier, K.J. (1990). The Wages of Sin: Taxing America's Legal Vices. *Western Political Quarterly*, 43: 577–595.

Johnson, P.M. (2000, March 3). Education, Gambling, and the Churches: Religious Denominationalism and Voter Mobilization Patterns in the 1999 Alabama Lottery Referendum. Paper presented at the Citadel Conference on Southern Politics, Charleston, S.C.

Joyce, K.M. (1979, Winter). Public Opinion and the Politics of Gambling. *Journal of Social Issues*, 35: 144–165.

Katz, A. (1989, May 1). Louisiana Voters Want a Lottery, Pollsters Say. *Times-Picayune*, p. A5.

Keating, S. (1994, August 24). Video Poker's Profits Flush State Blind to Illicit Gaming. *Denver Post* [Online]. Available: http://www.news library.com.

Keating, Stephen. (1994, September 30). Commission Cuts Gaming Tax to Aid Smaller Casinos. *Denver Post* [Online]. Available: http://www. newslibrary.com/.

Kelly, J.M. (1997). American Indian Gaming Law. In W.R. Eadington and J.A. Cornelius (Eds.), *Gambling: Public Policies and the Social Sciences.* Reno: University of Nevada.

Kentucky Gambling Study Shows State Loses Funds. (1999, December 17). *Las Vegas Review-Journal.* [Online] Available: http://www.lvrj.com/ lvrj_home/1999/Dec-17-Fri-1999/business/12575857.html.

Kindt, J.W. (1998, March). Follow the Money: Gambling, Ethics, and Subpoenas. *Annals of the American Academy of Political and Social Science*, 556: 85–97.

King, L. (1994). An Overview of Mississippi Gaming Legislation and Local Activities. Working Paper 9041. Jackson, MS: Center for Policy Research and Planning.

King, W. (1993, January 30). Postponement of New Keno Game Sought by New Jersey Governor. *New York Times*, p. 28.

Knickerbocker, B. (1999, June 7). The Growing Cost of Gambling. *Christian Science Monitor*, 11.

Kolko, G. (1965). *Railroads and Regulation: 1877–1916.* Princeton, NJ: Princeton University Press.

Koselka, R., & Palmeri, C. (1993, May). Snake Eyes. *Forbes,* 151: 13–17.

Koughan, M. (1997, July/August). Easy Money. *Mother Jones.* 35, 5–9.

Lambrecht, B., & Poor, T. (1997, February 13). Gephardt Names Union Official to Gaming Panel. *(St. Louis) Post-Dispatch,* p. 2.

Lane, G. (2000, July 20). Colorado Casinos Take in Record $52.8 Million Profit in June. *Denver Post* [Online]. Available: http://ehostvgw 14.2pn . . . /fulltext.asp.

Larsen, M.D. (1995). Gaming Industry Development: A Comparison of Three States. *Economic Development Review,* 13(4): 4–9.

Lasswell, H. (1971). *A Pre-View of Policy Sciences.* New York: American Elsevier.

Lesieur, H.R. (1984). *The Chase: Career of the Compulsive Gambler.* Cambridge, MA: Schenkman.

Lesieur, H.R. (1998). Costs and Treatment of Pathological Gambling. *Annals of the American Academy of Political and Social Science,* 556: 97–108.

Leven, C., Phares, D., & Louishomme, C. (1998). *The Economic Impact of Gaming in Missouri.* St. Louis, MO: Civic Progress Association.

Lorenz, V.C., & Yaffee, R.A. (1986). Pathological Gambling: Psychosomatic, Emotional and Marital Difficulties as Reported by the Gambler. *Journal of Gambling Behavior* 2: 40–49.

Lorenz, V. C., & Yaffee. R. A. (1987). Pathological Gambling: Psychosomatic, Emotional and Marital Difficulties as Reported by the Spouse. *Journal of Gambling Behavior* 3: 13–26.

Lorenz, V. C., & R. A. Yaffee. 1989. Pathological Gamblers and Their Spouses: Problems in Interaction, *Journal of Gambling Behavior,* 5: 113–126.

Lotteries. (1999). Staff Report Prepared for the National Gambling Impact Study Commission. Accessed January 12, 2001. Available: http://www.ngisc.com/reports/lotteries.html.

Lottery Backers Ready for Fight. (1973, April 16). *Chicago Tribune,* p. A5.

Lottery Vote Shows Power of Church. (1999, October 14). *Birmingham News,* p. 1.

Lowi, T. J. (1972). Four Systems of Policy, Politics, and Choice. *Public Administration Review,* 32: 298–310.

Lowi, T. J. (1988). New Dimensions in Policy and Politics. In R. Tatalovich & B. Daynes (Eds.), *Social Regulatory Policy* (pp. x–xxi). Boulder, CO: Westview.

Madden, M. (1991). *Gaming in South Dakota: A Statistical Description and Analysis of Its Socio-Economic Impacts.* Vermillion, SD: University of South Dakota.

Mason, John L., and Michael Nelson. (1999, September). The Politics of
    Gambling in the South. Paper presented at the 1999 Annual Meeting
    of the American Political Science Association, Atlanta, Georgia.

Massaro, G. (1990, November 30). Hopper: 'We're Not Going to Be a
    Copy of Deadwood.' *Denver Rocky Mountain News,* p. 2.

McConnell, G. (1966). *Private Power and American Democracy.* New York:
    Knopf.

McCullough, A. (1992). High Stakes Gambling at Indian Reservations. Pa-
    per presented at the 1992 Southern Political Science Association An-
    nual Meeting, Atlanta, GA.

McKinney, E.B., & Swain, J.W. (1993). State Lotteries: Explaining Their
    Popularity. *International Journal of Public Administration,* 16:
    1023–1035.

Meier, K.J. (1988). *The Political Economy of Regulation: The Case of Insur-
    ance.* Albany: State University of New York Press.

Meier, K.J. (1994). *The Politics of Sin.* Armonk, NY: M.E. Sharpe.

Meier, K.J. (1999). Sex, Drugs, Rock, and Roll: A Theory of Morality Pol-
    itics. *Policy Studies Journal,* 27(4), 681–695.

Meier, K. J. (2001). Drugs, Sex, and Rock and Roll: A Theory of Morality
    Politics. In C.Z. Mooney (Ed.), *The Public Clash of Private Values:
    The Politics of Morality Policy* (pp. 21–36). New York, NY: Chatham
    House.

Meier, K. J., & Johnson, C. M. (1990). The Politics of Demon Rum: Reg-
    ulating Alcohol and Its Deleterious Consequences. *American Politics
    Quarterly,* 18(4): 404–429.

Meier, K.J., & McFarlane, D.R. (1992). State Policies on Funding Abor-
    tions: A Pooled Time Series Analysis. *Social Science Quarterly,* 73(3):
    690–698.

Meyer-Arendt, K. (1995). Casino Gaming in Mississippi: Location, Loca-
    tion, Location. *Economic Development Review,* 13: 27–33.

Miller, W.J., & Schwartz, M.D. (1998). Casinos and Street Crime. *Amer-
    ican Academy of Political and Social Science,* 556: 124–137.

Minor, Bill. (1989, November 8). Gaming Commission, Gambling in the
    Sound before the Legislature. *The Biloxi (Mississippi) Sun-Herald,*
    p. A1.

"Mississippi." (1990, January 8). *USA Today,* p. 8A.

Mississippi Gaming Commission. (2001). *Casino Gross Gaming Revenues*
    [Online]. Available: http://www.msgaming.com.

Mixon, F.G., Caudill, S.B., Ford, J.M., & Peng, T. C. (1997). The Rise (or
    Fall) of Lottery Adoption Within the Logic of Collective Action:
    Some Empirical Evidence. *Journal of Economics and Finance,* 21(1):
    43–49.

Moehring, E.P. (1989). *Resort City in the Sunbelt: Las Vegas 1930–1970.*
    Reno: University of Nevada Press.

Mooney, C.Z., ed. (2001). *The Public Clash of Private Values*. New York: Chatham House.

Mooney, C.Z., & Lee, M.-H. (1995). Legislating Morality in the American States: The Case of Pre-Roe Abortion Regulation Reform. *American Journal of Political Science*, 39(3): 599–627.

Mooney, C.Z., & Lee, M.-H. (1999a, November). Morality Policy Reinvention: State Death Penalties. *Annals of the American Academy of Political and Social Sciences*, 566: 80–92.

Mooney, C.Z., & Lee, M.-H. (1999b). The Temporal Diffusion of Morality Policy: The Case of Death Penalty Legislation in the American States. *Policy Studies Journal*, 27(4): 766–781.

Mooney, C.Z., & Lee, M.-H. (2000). The Influence of Values on Consensus and Contentious Morality Policy: U.S. Death Penalty Reform, 1956–83. *Journal of Politics*, 62(1): 223–239.

Mylchrest, I. (2001). Avoiding the Issue Down Under: The Politics of Legalizing Abortion in Australia. In C. Mooney (Ed.), *The Public Clash of Private Values* (pp. 227–244). New York: Chatham House.

National Gambling Impact Study Commission. (1999). Final Report [Online]. Available: http://www.ngisc.com.

National Opinion Research Center. (1999). Gambling Behavior and Impact Study Prepared for the National Gambling Impact Study Commission [Online]. Available: http://www.icpsr.umich.edu/SAMHDA/studies.html.

Newman, O. (1972). *Gambling: Hazard and Reward*. London: Athlone.

Nice, D.C. (1992). The States and the Death Penalty. *Western Political Quarterly*, 45(4): 1037–1048.

Norrander, B., & Wilcox, C. (1999). Public Policymaking in the States: The Case of Post-Roe Abortion Policy. *Policy Studies Journal*, 27(4): 61–89.

Norrander, B., & Wilcox, C. (2001). Public Opinion and Policymaking in the States: The Case of Post-Roe Abortion Policy. In C. Mooney (Ed.), *The Public Clash of Private Values* (pp.143–159). New York: Chatham House.

Nossiter, A. (1996, November 19). Ballots Trim Gambling's Lucky Run. *New York Times*, p. A9.

O'Brien, T.L. (1998). *Bad Bet: The Inside Story of the Glamour, Glitz, and Danger of America's Gambling Industry*. New York: Times Books.

Officials Visit Deadwood for Insight into Gambling. (1990, November 30). *Denver Rocky Mountain News*, p. 2.

Olson, M., Jr. (1965). *The Logic of Collective Action*. Cambridge, MA: Harvard University Press.

Outshoorn, J. (1996). The Stability of Compromise: Abortion Politics in Western Europe. In M. Githens & D. M. Stetson (Eds.), *Abortion*

Politics: Public Policy in Cross-Country Perspective (pp. 145–165). London: Routledge.

Palermo, D. (1997, August 1). Casinos Energize Coast Economy. *The Biloxi (Mississippi) Sun-Herald*, p. A1.

Palermo, D. (1998, August 23). The Day Gambling Died. *The Biloxi (Mississippi) Sun-Herald*, p. A1.

Pathological Gambling: A Critical Review. (1999). Committee on the Social and Economic Impact of Pathological Gambling, National Research Council of the National Academy of Sciences.

Patriquin, R. (1994, February 13). Track Owner Plans Gambling Expansion. *Mobile (Alabama) Register*, p. A1.

Paying the Price: How Special Interests Block Common Sense Solutions. (2000). *Common Cause* [Online] Available: http://www.common cause.org/publications/price/gambling.htm.

PEER Committee. (1996). *A Review of the Adequacy of the MS Gaming Commission's Regulation.* Jackson: Mississippi Legislature.

Pierce, P.A., & Miller, D.E. (2001). Variation in the Diffusion of State Lottery Adoptions: How Revenue Dedication Changes Morality Politics. In Mooney, C.Z. (Ed.), *The Public Clash of Private Values: The Politics of Morality Policy* (pp. 160–169). New York: Chatham House.

Pierce, P.A., & Miller, D.E. (1999). Variations in the Diffusion of State Lottery Adoptions: How Revenue Dedication Changes Morality Politics. *Policy Studies Journal*, 27(4): 696–706.

Pirog-Good, M. & Mikesell, J. L. (1995). Longitudinal Evidence of the Changing Socio-Economic Profile of a State Lottery Market. *Policy Studies Journal*, 23: 451–456.

Pollock, M. (1987). *Hostage to Fortune: Atlantic City and Casino Gambling.* Princeton, NJ: Center for Analysis of Public Issues.

Preston, F.W., Bernhard, B.J., Hunter, R.E., & Bybee, S.L. (1998, March). Gambling as Stigmatized Behavior: Regional Relabeling and the Law. *Annals of the American Academy of Political and Social Science*, 556: 186–196.

Pulley, B. (1998a, March 22). Casinos Increase Their Contributions to U.S. Campaigns. *New York Times*, p. 1.

Pulley, B. (1998b, March 22). A Gambling Impressario Leaves Little to Chance. *New York Times*, p. 1.

Reardon, P.T. (1993, October 13). Casino Backers Fail to Persuade Voters. *Chicago Tribune*, p. 2C.

Rivenbark, W.C., & Rounsaville, B.B. (1996). The Incidence of Casino Gaming Taxes in Mississippi: Setting the Stage. *Public Administration Quarterly*, 19(2): 129–142.

Riverboats Haven't Sunk Lottery Revenues (1995, June 28). *The Chicago Tribune*, p. 1A.

Rolston, B., & Eggert, A. (Eds.). (1994). *Abortion in the New Europe*. Westport, CT: Greenwood.

Rose, I.N. (1991). *The Rise and Fall of Legal Gambling*. Reno: University of Nevada Press.

Rose, I.N. (1996). Legal Gambling's Historic Triumph at the Polls. *Gambling and the Law*, No. 105. Los Angeles, CA: Author.

Rose, I.N. (1999). Report to the National Gambling Impact Study Commission [Online]. Available: http://www.ngisc.gov.

Rose, I.N. (2000, November 26). Status of Gaming Enabling Laws. Gambling and the Law [Online]. Available: http://www.gamblingandthelaw.com

Ryan, T.P., & Speyrer, J.F. (1999). *Gambling in Louisiana: A Cost Benefit Analysis*. New Orleans, LA: University of New Orleans.

Sanko, J. (1989, October 14). Colorado Lottery's Luck Running Hot, Cold in Ticket Sales. *Denver Rocky Mountain News* [Online]. Available: http://archives.rockymountain.news.com.

Schmidt, W.E. (1984, June 25). Voters Approve Thoroughbreds. *New York Times*, p. 10.

Shaffer, H.J., & Hall, M.N. (1996). Estimating the Prevalence of Adolescent Gambling Disorders: A Quantitative Synthesis and Guide toward Standard Gambling Nomenclature. *Journal of Gambling Studies*, 12: 193–214.

Shaffer, H.J., Hall, M.N., & Vander Bilt, J. (1997). Estimating the Prevalence of Disordered Gambling Behavior in the United States and Canada: A Meta-Analysis. Paper prepared for the National Center for Responsible Gambling, Kansas City, Missouri.

Shaffer, H.J., Stein, S.A., Gambino, B., & Cummings, T.N. (1989). *Compulsive Gambling: Theory, Research, and Practice*. Lexington, MA: Lexington Books.

Shapiro, J.P. (1996, January 15). America's Gambling Fever. *U.S. News & World Report*, 126, (2), 52–61.

Sharp, E.B. (1997). A Comparative Anatomy of Urban Social Conflict. *Political Research Quarterly*, 50(2), 261–280.

Siegelman, Aides, Ponder Loss. (1999, October 14). *Birmingham News*, p. 1.

Siegelman and Lottery Win Big. (1998, November 10). *Gannett News* [Online]. Available: http://www.gannett.com.

Simon, H. A. (1958). *Administrative Behavior*. New York: Free Press.

Simon, P. (1995, July 31). *The Explosive Growth of Gambling in the United States. Speech before the 104th Congress*. Washington, DC: Congressional Record.

Simpson, J. (2001, July 7). Criticism of Gaming Thick at Town Meeting. *Las Vegas Review Journal*, p. 3.

Skolnick, J.H. (1978). *House of Cards: The Legalization and Control of Casino Gambling.* Boston: Little, Brown, & Company.

Smith, K. (1997, August). Storytelling, Sympathy, and Moral Judgment in American Abolitionism. Paper presented at the annual meeting of the American Political Science Association, Washington, DC.

Smith, K.B. (1999). Clean Thoughts and Dirty Minds: The Politics of Porn. *Policy Studies Journal,* 27(4): 723–734.

Smith, K.B. (2001). Clean Thoughts and Dirty Minds: The Politics of Porn. In C. Mooney (Ed.), *The Public Clash of Private Values* (pp.187–200). New York: Chatham House.

Statement of Senator Carl Levin Permanent Subcommitte on Investigations Hearing on Securities Fraud on the Internet. March 22, 1999. Available at: http://levin.senate.gov/floor/032299.htm.

State's Mood Shifts on Casinos. (1993, May 30). *Chicago Tribune,* p. 6A.

Steele, D.R. (1997, September). *Yes, Gambling Is Productive and Rational.* Port Townsend, WA: Liberty Magazine.

Sternlieb, G., & Hughes, J. W. (1983.) *The Atlantic City Gamble.* Cambridge, MA: Harvard University Press.

Stinchfield, R., & Winters, K. (1998, March). Gambling and Problem Gambling among Youths. *Annals of the American Academy of Political and Social Science,* 556: 172–185.

Stokowski, P.A. (1996). *Riches and Regrets: Betting on Gambling in Two Colorado Mountain Towns.* Niwot, CO: University Press of Colorado.

Stone, D. (1997). *Policy Paradox: The Art of Political Decision Making.* New York: Norton.

Stone, P.H. (1998, June 6). Upping the Ante. *National Journal,* 1288–1292.

Studlar, D.T. (2001). What Constitutes Morality Policy? A Cross-National Analysis. In C. Mooney (Ed.), *The Public Clash of Private Values* (pp. 37–54). New York: Chatham House.

Suits, D.B. (1977). Gambling Taxes: Regressivity and Revenue Potential. *National Tax Journal,* 30: 25–33.

Sutphen, S., Grant, R. M., & Ball, B. (1994, March). Upping the Ante: Gambling as a Revenue Source for Local Governments. *Southeastern Political Review,* 22: 77–96.

Szymanski, A.M. (1997, August). Dry Compulsions: Prohibition and the Creation of State-Level Enforcement Agencies. Paper presented at the annual meeting of the American Political Science Association, Washington, DC.

Tatalovich, R., & Daynes, B.W. (Eds.). (1988). *Social Regulatory Policymaking—Moral Controversies in American Politics.* Boulder, CO: Westview.

Tatalovich, R., Smith, T.A., & Bobic, M.P. (1994). Moral Conflict and the Policy Process. *Policy Currents*, 4(4): 3–6.

Thalheimer, R., & Ali, M.M. (1995). The Demand for Parimutuel Horse Race Wagering and Attendance. *Management Science*, 4(1): 129–136.

Thomas, E. (1985, March 11). Taking a Louisiana Mud Bath. *Time*, 29.

Thompson Cuts Secret Deal for Kenosha Casino. (1999). *Gambling Magazine.Com* Available at: http://www.gamblingmagazine.com/articles/14/14-1002.htm.

Thompson Vows to Fight Land-Based Casino. (1992, October 16). *Chicago Tribune*, 1-D.

Thompson, W.N. (1994). *Legalized Gambling*. Santa Barbara, CA: ABC–CLIO.

Thompson, W. N., & Dever, D. (1997). Gambling Enterprise and the Restoration of Native American Sovereignty. In W. R. Eadington & J. Cornelius (Eds.), *Gambling Public Policies and the Social Sciences* (pp. 295–318). Reno, NV: Institute for the Study of Gambling and Commercial Gaming.

Thompson, W. N., & Gazel, R. (1997). The Last Resort Revisited: The Spread of Gambling as a "Prisoner's Dilemma." In W.R. Eadington & J. Cornelius (Eds.), *Gambling Public Policies and the Social Sciences* (pp. 183–206). Reno, NV: Institute for the Study of Gambling and Commercial Gaming.

Thompson, W.N., Gazel, R., & Rickman, D. (1995, April). *Casinos & Crime in Wisconsin: What's the Connection?* Milwaukee: Wisconsin Policy Research Institute.

Thompson, W.N., Gazel, R., & Rickman, D. (1996, July). *The Social Costs of Gambling in Wisconsin*. Wisconsin Policy Research Institute.

Tribal Gaming." Colorado Gaming Commission. (2001). Overview [Online]. Available: http://www.gaming.state.co.us.

Truitt, L.J. (1997). The Regulation and Economic Impact of Riverboat Casino Gaming in Illinois. In W.R. Eadington & J. Cornelius (Eds.), *Gambling Public Policies and the Social Sciences* (pp. 127–150). Reno, NV: Institute for the Study of Gambling and Commercial Gaming.

Trump's Michelangelo. (1996, April 4). *New York Times*, p. 4.

Tunica Convention and Visitors Bureau. (1999, September 9). Strategic Action Plan for Tourism in Tunica County, Mississippi. Unpublished report prepared by Pricewaterhouse Coopers, LLP.

Turner, W.B. (1993). What the Numbers Say: An Analytical Look at Gaming's Performance. *International Gaming and Wagering Business*, 14: 62–63.

Uniform Code of Louisiana. (1994).

United Methodist Discipline. (2000). General Board of Discipline of the United Methodist Church, Nashville, TN: General Board.

Vergari, S. (2001). Morality Politics and the Implementation of Abstinence-Only Sex Education: A Case of Policy Compromise. In C. Mooney (Ed.), *The Public Clash of Private Values* (pp. 201–212). New York: Chatham House.

Volberg, R.A. (1996). Gambling & Problem Gambling in Mississippi. Study prepared for the Mississippi Council on Problem Gambling. [Online] Available: http://msgambler.org/.

von Herrmann, D.K. (1997) *The States' Biggest Gamble: Are Public Opinion and Competition Shaping American State Gambling Policy?* Unpublished doctoral dissertation, University of Alabama, Tuscaloosa.

von Herrmann, D.K. (1998). Why States Gamble on Gambling Revenue: A Comparative Case Study Approach. *Comparative State Politics*, 19(5): 33–46.

von Herrmann, D.K. (1999). The Decision to Legalize Gambling: A Model of Why States Do What They Do. *International Journal of Public Administration*, 22(11 & 12): 1659–1680.

von Herrmann, D. K., Ingram, R., & Smith, W. (2000, June 30). Gaming in the Mississippi Economy. Study prepared for the Board of Trustees of the State Institutions of Higher Learning. Available: http://www-org.usm.edu/~ccedev/Gamingstudy.pdf.

The Wager (Weekly Addiction Gambling Education Report of the Division on Addictions at Harvard Medical School). (2000, May 23). *The Roper Files* [Online]. Available: http://www.thewager.org.

Wald. K.D. (1997). *Religion and Politics in the United States* (3rd ed.). Washington, DC: Congressional Quarterly Press.

Walker, D.M., & Barnett, A.H. (1999). The Social Costs of Gambling: An Economic Perspective. *Journal of Gambling Studies*, 15: 181–212.

Walker, J.L. (1969, September). The Diffusion of Innovations among the American States. *American Political Science Review*, 63: 880–899.

Walker, J.L. (1973). Comment: Problems in Research on the Diffusion of Policy Innovations. *American Political Science Review*, 67: 1186–1191.

Walston, J. (1994, June 26). Has the Gamble Paid Off? *Atlanta Journal Constitution* [Online]. Available: http://www.ajc.com.

Walton. V. (2000, February 15). Greene Co. Video Poker Lawsuit Settled. *The Birmingham (Alabama) News*, p. A2.

Weber, P.J., & Jones, W.L. (1994). *U.S. Religious Interest Groups: Institutional Profiles*. Westport, CT: Greenwood.

Weinstein D., & Deitch, L. (1974). *The Impact of Legalized Gambling: The Socioeconomic Consequences of Lotteries and Off-Track Betting*. New York: Praeger.

"What's News?" (1998, January 7). *Las Vegas Review Journal*, 4.

White, K. (1996, May 3). Casino Interests Hire Big Names to Shape Gambling Study Commission. *Gannett News Service* [Online]. Available: http://www.gannett.com/.

Winn, M., & Whicker, M.L. (1989). Indicators of State Lottery Adoptions. *Policy Studies Journal*, 18: 293–305.

Winters, K., Stinchfield, R., & Fulkerson, J. (1993). Patterns and Characteristics of Adolescent Gambling. *Journal of Gambling Studies*, 9: 371–386.

Wohlenberg, E.H. (1992). Recent U.S. Gambling Legalization: A Case Study of Lotteries. *Social Science Journal*, 29: 167–184.

Wolf, F.R. (1995, October 3). A Close Look at Gambling. *Washington Post*, p. A19.

Worsham, J. (1997). *Other People's Money: Policy Change, Congress, and Bank Regulation*. Boulder, CO: Westview.

Yardley, J. (1993, May 4). Hobson's City Gamble. *Atlanta Journal Consitution*, p. M1.

Zimring, F.E., & Hawkins, G. (1986). *Capital Punishment and the American Agenda*. New York: Cambridge University Press.

Zola, I.K. (1963). Observations on Gambling in a Lower Class Setting. *Social Problems*, 10(4): 353–361.

Index

About the Author

DENISE VON HERRMANN is Chair of the Arts and Sciences Division, the University of Southern Mississippi, Gulf Coast.